2024

Air Fryer

Cookbook for Busy Beginners UK

2000+ Days of   Easy, Mouthwatering & Quick Recipes

Book incl. Side Dishes, Snacks, Desserts & More -

Ready In Less Than 30 Minutes

• Radka Janoscova •

Copyright © 2024 by Radka Janoscova

All rights reserved worldwide.

No portion of this work may be reproduced or transmitted in any form or by any means, electronic or mechanical, including photocopying, recording, or any information retrieval system, without the prior written permission of the publisher, except for brief quotations used in critical reviews.

Legal Disclaimer:

This material is protected by copyright law and is intended solely for personal use. Any unauthorized distribution, resale, or utilization of the content contained herein is strictly prohibited and may lead to legal action.

Warning and Disclaimer:

The content presented in this work is provided for educational and entertainment purposes only. While every effort has been made to ensure its accuracy and reliability, no warranties, express or implied, are provided. The author does not offer legal, financial, medical, or professional advice. By accessing this material, the reader acknowledges that the author and publisher are not liable for any direct or indirect losses resulting from the utilization of the information presented herein, including but not limited to errors or omissions.

Furthermore, readers are advised to exercise caution and discretion when applying the concepts discussed in this work to their personal or professional lives. It is recommended to seek guidance from appropriate experts or professionals before making significant decisions based on the contents herein. The author and publisher disclaim any responsibility for any unfavorable outcomes arising from the application of the ideas, recommendations, or strategies outlined in this work.

Table of Contents

Introduction 2

    Air Fryer: Redefining Culinary Excellence 2

    Why Air Fryers Have Gained Popularity 2

    Tips for Air Fryer Beginners 3

    Air Fryer Maintenance and Care: Essential Tips for Longevity 3

Chapter 1 Breakfasts 5

Chapter 2 Family Favorites 14

Chapter 3 Fast and Easy Everyday Favourites 18

Chapter 4 Poultry 21

Chapter 5 Beef, Pork, and Lamb 33

Chapter 6 Fish and Seafood 45

Chapter 7 Snacks and Starters 56

Chapter 8 Vegetables and Sides 64

Chapter 9 Vegetarian Mains 72

Chapter 10 Desserts 76

Appendix: Recipe Index 80

Introduction

Get ready to revolutionize your kitchen and reimagine the way you cook with the ultimate companion: the Air Fryer Cookbook. Prepare to embark on a culinary adventure like no other, where deliciousness meets healthiness in every bite.

Imagine savoring all your favorite fried foods—crispy fries, crunchy chicken tenders, and golden onion rings—without the guilt of excess oil. With the Air Fryer Cookbook by your side, this dream becomes a mouthwatering reality.

But this cookbook isn't just about recipes; it's a treasure trove of culinary wisdom and innovation. Delve into a world of flavor as we guide you through essential air frying techniques, optimal cooking times, and creative flavor combinations that will tantalize your taste buds.

At the heart of our cookbook lies the air fryer itself—a true kitchen superhero. Say goodbye to messy, unhealthy frying methods and hello to a cleaner, healthier way of cooking. With minimal to no oil, you'll achieve that irresistible crispiness without sacrificing flavor or texture.

But the magic doesn't stop there. Prepare to be amazed by the versatility of your air fryer as we explore a diverse range of recipes, from appetizers and mains to desserts and snacks. With our easy-to-follow instructions and mouthwatering photography, you'll be whipping up gourmet meals in no time.

So, are you ready to embark on a journey to culinary excellence? Let the Air Fryer Cookbook be your guide as we unlock the full potential of air frying together. Whether you're a seasoned chef or a kitchen novice, prepare to be inspired, amazed, and utterly satisfied with every dish you create. It's time to elevate your cooking game and make healthy eating a delicious pleasure.

Air Fryer: Redefining Culinary Excellence

What is an Air Fryer?

Air fryers have surged in popularity, but what exactly are they? Imagine a compact convection oven resting on your countertop. Instead of submerging your food in hot oil like a traditional deep fryer, an air fryer utilizes circulating hot air to cook your meals to crispy perfection. By eschewing excessive oil, air fryers significantly reduce the fat content in your food—up to 75 percent less compared to traditional frying methods.

Moreover, air fryers aren't limited to just frying; they excel at grilling, roasting, and baking a diverse array of dishes. From succulent chicken wings to perfectly roasted vegetables and even indulgent desserts like donuts and brownies, the possibilities are endless. Additionally, they produce minimal smoke and odor, making them a convenient and efficient option for indoor cooking.

The History of Air Fryers

Though air fryers may seem like a modern invention, their roots trace back to the 1940s when French engineers pioneered the concept of cooking with hot air. However, it wasn't until 2010 that the first air fryer hit the market, albeit with basic features and limited capacity. Since then, advancements in technology have transformed air fryers into indispensable kitchen appliances, available in various sizes and with an array of features to suit different culinary needs.

Why Air Fryers Have Gained Popularity

Air fryers have become kitchen staples worldwide, thanks to their myriad benefits:

Healthier Cooking: With minimal to no oil required,

air fryers offer a healthier alternative to traditional frying methods, making them ideal for calorie-conscious individuals.

Versatility: From savory delights to sweet treats, air fryers can handle a wide range of dishes, with some models even offering accessories for added cooking versatility.

Convenience: With simple controls and quick cooking times, air fryers make meal preparation a breeze, ensuring delicious and nutritious meals in no time.

Crispy Texture: Enjoy the satisfying crunch of fried food without the excess oil, thanks to the hot air circulation of air fryers.

Easy to Clean: Most air fryers feature removable, non-stick components that are dishwasher safe, making cleanup a breeze.

Reduced Odor: Say goodbye to lingering cooking odors, as air fryers produce less smoke and odor compared to traditional frying methods.

Space-Saving Design: Compact and efficient, air fryers take up minimal counter space, making them an ideal choice for smaller kitchens or living spaces.

In conclusion, air fryers have revolutionized the culinary landscape, offering a healthier, more convenient, and versatile approach to cooking. Whether you're whipping up a quick snack or preparing a gourmet feast, an air fryer is sure to elevate your culinary experience to new heights.

Tips for Air Fryer Beginners

If you're new to using an air fryer, here are some essential tips to help you master this versatile kitchen appliance and achieve delicious results every time:

Preheat for Success:

Similar to an oven, preheating your air fryer is crucial for optimal cooking results. This step ensures even heat distribution and helps achieve that desirable crispy texture.

Mind the Space:

Avoid overcrowding the air fryer basket or tray. Leaving adequate space between food items allows for proper air circulation, preventing uneven cooking and soggy outcomes.

Shake It Up:

Halfway through the cooking process, shake the basket or tray to redistribute the food. This simple step promotes uniform cooking by exposing all sides of the food to the circulating hot air.

Embrace a Hint of Oil:

While air frying typically requires minimal to no oil, adding a light coating can enhance flavor and texture. Consider using a spray bottle to evenly distribute a small amount of oil over your food before cooking.

Experiment and Adjust:

Each air fryer model operates differently, so don't hesitate to experiment with various temperatures and cooking times. Start with the recommended settings in your air fryer manual and adjust as needed based on your preferences and results.

Keep It Clean:

Regular maintenance is key to keeping your air fryer in top condition. After each use, wipe down the basket and tray, and follow the manufacturer's instructions for deep cleaning to ensure peak performance.

By incorporating these tips into your air frying routine, you'll be well-equipped to unleash the full potential of your air fryer and create mouthwatering, crispy meals with ease. Happy air frying!

Air Fryer Maintenance and Care: Essential Tips for Longevity

To keep your air fryer operating smoothly and

consistently delivering delicious meals, it's crucial to prioritize its maintenance. Here are some expert tips to ensure your air fryer stays in top condition:

Clean After Every Use:

After each cooking session, take a moment to clean the basket and tray. Wipe them down with a damp cloth or sponge to remove any food residue, ensuring they are completely dry before storing.

Schedule Deep Cleaning:

Depending on frequency of use, aim to deep clean your air fryer every few weeks or months. Refer to the manufacturer's instructions for specific cleaning guidelines and recommendations tailored to your model.

Choose Gentle Cleaners:

Opt for non-abrasive cleaners when tidying up your air fryer. Avoid harsh chemicals or abrasive scrubbers that could potentially damage the appliance's surface. Instead, use a mild dish soap and a soft sponge or cloth for safe and effective cleaning.

Mind the Water:

While cleaning, never immerse the entire appliance in water. Air fryers are not designed to be submerged, so focus on cleaning only the exterior and removable parts.

Store with Care:

When your air fryer isn't in use, store it in a cool, dry place to prevent damage and maintain its functionality. Avoid stacking heavy items on top of it or placing it near heat sources that could potentially affect its performance.

Address Damage Promptly:

If you notice any signs of damage or wear on your air fryer, address them promptly. Replace damaged parts as soon as possible to prevent further deterioration and ensure optimal performance.

By adhering to these maintenance tips, you can prolong the lifespan of your air fryer and continue enjoying crispy, flavorful meals for years to come. With proper care and attention, your air fryer will remain a reliable kitchen companion, ready to elevate your culinary creations whenever you need it.

Chapter 1 Breakfasts

Mississippi Spice Muffins

Prep time: 15 minutes | Cook time: 13 minutes | Makes 12 muffins

1 kg plain

1 tablespoon ground cinnamon

2 teaspoons baking soda

2 teaspoons allspice

1 teaspoon ground cloves

1 teaspoon salt

235 g (2 sticks) butter, room temperature

350 g sugar

2 large eggs, lightly beaten

475 ml unsweetened apple sauce

60 g chopped pecans

1 to 2 tablespoons oil

1. In a large bowl, whisk the flour, cinnamon, baking soda, allspice, cloves, and salt until blended. 2. In another large bowl, combine the butter and sugar. Using an electric mixer, beat the mixture for 2 to 3 minutes until light and fluffy. Add the beaten eggs and stir until blended. 3. Add the flour mixture and apple sauce, alternating between the two and blending after each addition. Stir in the pecans. 4. Preheat the air fryer to 160ºC. Spritz 12 silicone muffin cups with oil. 5. Pour the batter into the prepared muffin cups, filling each halfway. Place the muffins in the air fryer basket. 6. Air fry for 6 minutes. Shake the basket and air fry for 7 minutes more. The muffins are done when a toothpick inserted into the middle comes out clean.

Golden Avocado Tempura

Prep time: 5 minutes | Cook time: 10 minutes | Serves 4

60 g bread crumbs

½ teaspoons salt

1 Haas avocado, pitted, peeled and sliced

Liquid from 1 tin white beans

1. Preheat the air fryer to 180 ºC. 2. Mix the bread crumbs and salt in a shallow bowl until well-incorporated. 3. Dip the avocado slices in the bean liquid, then into the bread crumbs. 4. Put the avocados in the air fryer, taking care not to overlap any slices, and air fry for 10 minutes, giving the basket a good shake at the halfway point. 5. Serve immediately.

Apple Cider Doughnut Holes

Prep time: 10 minutes | Cook time: 6 minutes | Makes 10 mini doughnuts

Doughnut Holes:

175 g plain flour

2 tablespoons granulated sugar

2 teaspoons baking powder

1 teaspoon baking soda

½ teaspoon coarse or flaky salt

Pinch of freshly grated nutmeg

60 ml plus 2 tablespoons buttermilk, chilled

2 tablespoons apple cider or apple juice, chilled

1 large egg, lightly beaten

Vegetable oil, for brushing

Glaze:

96 g icing sugar

2 tablespoons unsweetened apple sauce

¼ teaspoon vanilla extract

Pinch of coarse or flaky salt

1. Make the doughnut holes: In a bowl, whisk together the flour, granulated sugar, baking powder, baking soda, salt, and nutmeg until smooth. Add the buttermilk, cider, and egg and stir with a small rubber spatula or spoon until the dough just comes together. 2. Using a 28 g ice cream scoop or 2 tablespoons, scoop and drop 10 balls of dough into the air fryer basket, spaced evenly apart, and brush the tops lightly with oil. Air fry at 180°C until the doughnut holes are golden brown and fluffy, about 6 minutes. Transfer the doughnut holes to a wire rack to cool completely. 3. Make the glaze: In a small bowl, stir together the icing sugar, apple sauce, vanilla, and salt until smooth. 4. Dip the tops of the doughnuts holes in the glaze, then let stand until the glaze sets before serving. If you're impatient and want warm doughnuts, have the glaze ready to go while the doughnuts cook, then use the glaze as a dipping sauce for the warm doughnuts, fresh out of the air fryer.

Green Eggs and Gammon

Prep time: 5 minutes | Cook time: 10 minutes | Serves 2

1 large Hass avocado, halved and pitted

2 thin slices gammon

2 large eggs

2 tablespoons chopped spring onions, plus more for garnish

½ teaspoon fine sea salt

¼ teaspoon ground black pepper

60 g grated Cheddar cheese (omit for dairy-free)

1. Preheat the air fryer to 200°C. 2. Place a slice of gammon into the cavity of each avocado half. Crack an egg on top of the gammon, then sprinkle on the spring onions, salt, and pepper. 3. Place the avocado halves in the air fryer cut side up and air fry for 10 minutes, or until the egg is cooked to your desired doneness. Top with the cheese (if using) and air fry for 30 seconds

more, or until the cheese is melted. Garnish with chopped spring onions. 4. Best served fresh. Store extras in an airtight container in the fridge for up to 4 days. Reheat in a preheated 180°C air fryer for a few minutes, until warmed through.

Southwestern Gammon Egg Cups

Prep time: 5 minutes | Cook time: 12 minutes | Serves 2

4 (30 g) slices wafer-thin gammon

4 large eggs

2 tablespoons full-fat sour cream

60 g diced green pepper

2 tablespoons diced red pepper

2 tablespoons diced brown onion

120 g grated medium Cheddar cheese

1. Place one slice of gammon on the bottom of four baking cups. 2. In a large bowl, whisk eggs with sour cream. Stir in green pepper, red pepper, and onion. 3. Pour the egg mixture into gammon-lined baking cups. Top with Cheddar. Place cups into the air fryer basket. 4. Adjust the temperature to 160°C and bake for 12 minutes or until the tops are browned. 5. Serve warm.

Canadian Bacon Muffin Sandwiches

Prep time: 5 minutes | Cook time: 8 minutes | Serves 4

4 muffins, split

8 slices back bacon

4 slices cheese

Cooking spray

1. Preheat the air fryer to 190 ° C. 2. Make the sandwiches: Top each of 4 muffin halves with 2 slices of bacon, 1 slice of cheese, and finish with the remaining muffin half. 3. Put the sandwiches in the air

fryer basket and spritz the tops with cooking spray. 4. Bake for 4 minutes. Flip the sandwiches and bake for another 4 minutes. 5. Divide the sandwiches among four plates and serve warm.

Baked Potato Breakfast Boats

Prep time: 10 minutes | Cook time: 20 minutes | Serves 4

2 large white potatoes, scrubbed

rapeseed oil

Salt and freshly ground black pepper, to taste

4 eggs

2 tablespoons chopped, cooked bacon

235 g grated Cheddar cheese

1. Poke holes in the potatoes with a fork and microwave on full power for 5 minutes. 2. Turn potatoes over and cook an additional 3 to 5 minutes, or until the potatoes are fork-tender. 3. Cut the potatoes in half lengthwise and use a spoon to scoop out the inside of the potato. Be careful to leave a layer of potato so that it makes a sturdy "boat."4. Preheat the air fryer to 180 ° C. 5. Lightly spray the air fryer basket with rapeseed oil. Spray the skin side of the potatoes with oil and sprinkle with salt and pepper to taste. 6. Place the potato skins in the air fryer basket, skin-side down. Crack one egg into each potato skin. 7. Sprinkle ½ tablespoon of bacon pieces and 60 ml grated cheese on top of each egg. Sprinkle with salt and pepper to taste. 8. Air fry until the yolk is slightly runny, 5 to 6 minutes, or until the yolk is fully cooked, 7 to 10 minutes.

Breakfast Meatballs

Prep time: 10 minutes | Cook time: 15 minutes | Makes 18 meatballs

450 g pork banger meat, removed from casings

½ teaspoon salt

¼ teaspoon ground black pepper

120 g grated mature Cheddar cheese

30 g soft cheese, softened

1 large egg, whisked

1. Combine all ingredients in a large bowl. Form mixture into eighteen 1-inch meatballs. 2. Place meatballs into ungreased air fryer basket. Adjust the temperature to 200 ° C and air fry for 15 minutes, shaking basket three times during cooking. Meatballs will be browned on the outside and have an internal temperature of at least 64°C when completely cooked. Serve warm.

Tomato and Mozzarella Bruschetta

Prep time: 5 minutes | Cook time: 4 minutes | Serves 1

6 small loaf slices

120 g tomatoes, finely chopped

85 g Cheddar cheese, grated

1 tablespoon fresh basil, chopped

1 tablespoon rapeseed oil

1. Preheat the air fryer to 180°C. 2. Put the loaf slices inside the air fryer and air fry for about 3 minutes. 3. Add the tomato, Mozzarella, basil, and rapeseed oil on top. 4. Air fry for an additional minute before serving.

Not-So-English Muffins

Prep time: 5 minutes | Cook time: 10 minutes | Serves 4

2 strips turkey bacon, cut in half crosswise

2 whole-grain English muffins, split

235 ml fresh baby spinach, long stems removed

¼ ripe pear, peeled and thinly sliced

4 slices low-moisture Mozzarella or other melting cheese

1. Place bacon strips in air fryer basket and air fry at 200 °C for 2 minutes. Check and separate strips if necessary so they cook evenly. Cook for 3 to 4 more minutes, until crispy. Remove and drain on paper towels. 2. Place split muffin halves in air fryer basket and cook for 2 minutes, just until lightly browned. 3. Open air fryer and top each muffin with a quarter of the baby spinach, several pear slices, a strip of bacon, and a slice of cheese. 4. Air fry at 182 °C for 1 to 2 minutes, until cheese completely melts.

Mexican Breakfast Pepper Rings

Prep time: 5 minutes | Cook time: 10 minutes | Serves 4

rapeseed oil

1 large red, yellow, or orange pepper, cut into four ¾-inch rings

4 eggs

Salt and freshly ground black pepper, to taste

2 teaspoons tomato salsa

1. Preheat the air fryer to 180 °C. Lightly spray a baking pan with rapeseed oil. 2. Place 2 pepper rings on the pan. Crack one egg into each pepper ring. Season with salt and black pepper. 3. Spoon ½ teaspoon of tomato salsa on top of each egg. 4. Place the pan in the air fryer basket. Air fry until the yolk is slightly runny, 5 to 6 minutes or until the yolk is fully cooked, 8 to 10 minutes. 5. Repeat with the remaining 2 pepper rings. Serve hot.

Parmesan Banger Egg Muffins

Prep time: 5 minutes | Cook time: 20 minutes | Serves 4

170 g Italian-seasoned banger, sliced

6 eggs

30 ml double cream

Salt and ground black pepper, to taste

85 g Parmesan cheese, grated

1. Preheat the air fryer to 180ºC. Grease a muffin pan. 2. Put the sliced banger in the muffin pan. 3. Beat the eggs with the cream in a bowl and season with salt and pepper. 4. Pour half of the mixture over the bangers in the pan. 5. Sprinkle with cheese and the remaining egg mixture. 6. Bake in the preheated air fryer for 20 minutes or until set. 7. Serve immediately.

Bacon Eggs on the Go

Prep time: 5 minutes | Cook time: 15 minutes | Serves 1

2 eggs

110 g bacon, cooked

Salt and ground black pepper, to taste

1. Preheat the air fryer to 200ºC. Put liners in a regular cupcake tin. 2. Crack an egg into each of the cups and add the bacon. Season with some pepper and salt. 3. Bake in the preheated air fryer for 15 minutes, or until the eggs are set. Serve warm.

Egg Tarts

Prep time: 10 minutes | Cook time: 17 to 20 minutes | Makes 2 tarts

⅓ sheet frozen puff pastry, thawed

Cooking oil spray

120 g grated Cheddar cheese

2 eggs

¼ teaspoon salt, divided

1 teaspoon minced fresh parsley (optional)

1. Insert the crisper plate into the basket and the basket into the unit. Preheat the unit by selecting BAKE, setting the temperature to 200ºC, and setting the time to 3 minutes. Select START/STOP to begin. 2. Lay the puff pastry sheet on a piece of parchment paper and cut it in half. 3. Once the unit is preheated, spray the

crisper plate with cooking oil. Transfer the 2 squares of pastry to the basket, keeping them on the parchment paper. 4. Select BAKE, set the temperature to 200°C, and set the time to 20 minutes. Select START/STOP to begin. 5. After 10 minutes, use a metal spoon to press down the center of each pastry square to make a well. Divide the cheese equally between the baked pastries. Carefully crack an egg on top of the cheese, and sprinkle each with the salt. Resume cooking for 7 to 10 minutes. 6. When the cooking is complete, the eggs will be cooked through. Sprinkle each with parsley (if using) and serve.

Red Pepper and Feta Frittata

Prep time: 10 minutes | Cook time: 20 minutes | Serves 4

rapeseed oil cooking spray

8 large eggs

1 medium red pepper, diced

½ teaspoon salt

½ teaspoon black pepper

1 garlic clove, minced

120 g feta, divided

1. Preheat the air fryer to 180°C. Lightly coat the inside of a 6-inch round cake pan with rapeseed oil cooking spray. 2. In a large bowl, beat the eggs for 1 to 2 minutes, or until well combined. 3. Add the red pepper, salt, black pepper, and garlic to the eggs, and mix together until the red pepper is distributed throughout. 4. Fold in 60 ml the feta cheese. 5. Pour the egg mixture into the prepared cake pan, and sprinkle the remaining 60 ml feta over the top. 6. Place into the air fryer and bake for 18 to 20 minutes, or until the eggs are set in the center. 7. Remove from the air fryer and allow to cool for 5 minutes before serving.

Spinach and Bacon Roll-ups

Prep time: 5 minutes | Cook time: 8 to 9

minutes | Serves 4

4 wheat maize wraps (6- or 7-inch size)

4 slices Swiss cheese

235 g baby spinach leaves

4 slices turkey bacon

Special Equipment:

4 cocktail sticks, soak in water for at least 30 minutes

1. Preheat the air fryer to 200°C. 2. On a clean work surface, top each tortilla with one slice of cheese and 60 ml spinach, then tightly roll them up. 3. Wrap each tortilla with a strip of turkey bacon and secure with a toothpick. 4. Arrange the roll-ups in the air fryer basket, leaving space between each roll-up. 5. Air fry for 4 minutes. Flip the roll-ups with tongs and rearrange them for more even cooking. Air fry for another 4 to 5 minutes until the bacon is crisp. 6. Rest for 5 minutes and remove the cocktail sticks before serving.

Keto Quiche

Prep time: 10 minutes | Cook time: 1 hour | Makes 1 (6-inch) quiche

Crust:

150 g blanched almond flour

300 g grated Parmesan or Gouda cheese

¼ teaspoon fine sea salt

1 large egg, beaten

Filling:

120 g chicken or beef stock (or vegetable stock for vegetarian)

235 g grated Swiss cheese (about 110 g)

110 g soft cheese (120 ml)

1 tablespoon unsalted butter, melted

4 large eggs, beaten

80 g minced leeks or sliced spring onions

¾ teaspoon fine sea salt

⅛ teaspoon cayenne pepper

Chopped spring onions, for garnish

1. Preheat the air fryer to 160°C. Grease a pie dish. Spray two large pieces of parchment paper with avocado oil and set them on the countertop. 2. Make the crust: In a medium-sized bowl, combine the flour, cheese, and salt and mix well. Add the egg and mix until the dough is well combined and stiff. 3. Place the dough in the center of one of the greased pieces of parchment. Top with the other piece of parchment. Using a rolling pin, roll out the dough into a circle about 1/16 inch thick. 4. Press the pie crust into the prepared pie dish. Place it in the air fryer and bake for 12 minutes, or until it starts to lightly brown. 5. While the crust bakes, make the filling: In a large bowl, combine the stock, Swiss cheese, soft cheese, and butter. Stir in the eggs, leeks, salt, and cayenne pepper. When the crust is ready, pour the mixture into the crust. 6. Place the quiche in the air fryer and bake for 15 minutes. Turn the heat down to 150°C and bake for an additional 30 minutes, or until a knife inserted 1 inch from the edge comes out clean. You may have to cover the edges of the crust with foil to prevent burning. 7. Allow the quiche to cool for 10 minutes before garnishing it with chopped spring onions and cutting it into wedges. 8. Store leftovers in an airtight container in the refrigerator for up to 4 days or in the freezer for up to a month. Reheat in a preheated 180°C air fryer for a few minutes, until warmed through.

Eggnog Bread

Prep time: 10 minutes | Cook time: 18 minutes | Serves 6 to 8

120 g flour, plus more for dusting

35 g sugar

1 teaspoon baking powder

¼ teaspoon salt

¼ teaspoon nutmeg

120 ml eggnog

1 egg yolk

1 tablespoon plus 1 teaspoon butter, melted

60 g pecans

60 g chopped candied fruit (cherries, pineapple, or mixed fruits)

Cooking spray

1. Preheat the air fryer to 180°C 2.In a medium bowl, stir together the flour, sugar, baking powder, salt, and nutmeg 3.Add eggnog, egg yolk, and butter 4.Mix well but do not beat 5.Stir in nuts and fruit 6.Spray a baking dish with cooking spray and dust with flour 7.Spread batter into prepared pan and bake for 18 minutes or until top is dark golden brown and bread starts to pull away from sides of pan 8.Serve immediately.

Turkey Banger Breakfast Pizza

Prep time: 15 minutes | Cook time: 24 minutes | Serves 2

4 large eggs, divided

1 tablespoon water

½ teaspoon garlic powder

½ teaspoon onion granules

½ teaspoon dried oregano

2 tablespoons coconut flour

3 tablespoons grated Parmesan cheese

120 g grated low-moisture Mozzarella or other melting cheese

1 link cooked turkey banger, chopped (about 60 g)

2 sun-dried tomatoes, finely chopped

2 sping onions, thinly sliced

1. Preheat the air fryer to 200°C. Line a cake pan with

parchment paper and lightly coat the paper with rapeseed oil. 2. In a large bowl, whisk 2 of the eggs with the water, garlic powder, onion granules, and dried oregano. Add the coconut flour, breaking up any lumps with your hands as you add it to the bowl. Stir the coconut flour into the egg mixture, mixing until smooth. Stir in the Parmesan cheese. Allow the mixture to rest for a few minutes until thick and dough-like. 3. Transfer the mixture to the prepared pan. Use a spatula to spread it evenly and slightly up the sides of the pan. Air fry until the crust is set but still light in color, about 10 minutes. Top with the cheeses, banger, and sun-dried tomatoes. 4. Break the remaining 2 eggs into a small bowl, then slide them onto the pizza. Return the pizza to the air fryer. Air fry 10 to 14 minutes until the egg whites are set and the yolks are the desired doneness. Top with the spring onions and allow to rest for 5 minutes before serving.

Bacon, Broccoli and Cheese Bread Pudding

Prep time: 30 minutes | Cook time: 48 minutes | Serves 2 to 4

230 g streaky bacon, cut into ¼-inch pieces

700 g brioche bread or rolls, cut into ½-inch cubes

3 eggs

235 ml milk

½ teaspoon salt

freshly ground black pepper

235 g frozen broccoli florets, thawed and chopped

350 g grated Emmental cheese

1. Preheat the air fryer to 200°C. 2. Air fry the bacon for 6 to 10 minutes until crispy, shaking the basket a few times while it cooks to help it cook evenly. Remove the bacon and set it aside on a paper towel. 3. Air fry the brioche bread cubes for 2 minutes to dry and toast lightly. (If your brioche is a few days old and

slightly stale, you tin omit this step.) 4. Butter a cake pan. Combine all the ingredients in a large bowl and toss well. Transfer the mixture to the buttered cake pan, cover with aluminium foil and refrigerate the bread pudding overnight, or for at least 8 hours. 5. Remove the casserole from the refrigerator an hour before you plan to cook, and let it sit on the countertop to come to room temperature. 6. Preheat the air fryer to 170°C. Transfer the covered cake pan, to the basket of the air fryer, lowering the dish into the basket using a sling made of aluminium foil (fold a piece of aluminium foil into a strip about 2-inches wide by 24-inches long). Fold the ends of the aluminium foil over the top of the dish before returning the basket to the air fryer. Air fry for 20 minutes. Remove the foil and air fry for an additional 20 minutes. If the top starts to brown a little too much before the custard has set, simply return the foil to the pan. The bread pudding has cooked through when a skewer inserted into the center comes out clean.

Gluten-Free Muesli Cereal

Prep time: 7 minutes | Cook time: 30 minutes | Makes 820 ml

Oil, for spraying

350 g gluten-free porridge oats

120 g chopped walnuts

120 g chopped almonds

120 g pumpkin seeds

60 ml maple syrup or honey

1 tablespoon toasted sesame oil or vegetable oil

1 teaspoon ground cinnamon

½ teaspoon salt

120 g dried cranberries

1. Preheat the air fryer to 120°C. Line the air fryer basket with parchment and spray lightly with oil. (Do not skip the step of lining the basket; the parchment

will keep the muesli from falling through the holes.) 2. In a large bowl, mix together the oats, walnuts, almonds, pumpkin seeds, maple syrup, sesame oil, cinnamon, and salt. 3. Spread the mixture in an even layer in the prepared basket. 4. Cook for 30 minutes, stirring every 10 minutes. 5. Transfer the muesli to a bowl, add the dried cranberries, and toss to combine. 6. Let cool to room temperature before storing in an airtight container.

Bourbon Vanilla Eggy Bread

Prep time: 15 minutes | Cook time: 6 minutes | Serves 4

2 large eggs

2 tablespoons water

160 ml whole or semi-skimmed milk

1 tablespoon butter, melted

2 tablespoons bourbon

1 teaspoon vanilla extract

8 (1-inch-thick) French bread slices

Cooking spray

1. Preheat the air fryer to 160 °C. Line the air fryer basket with parchment paper and spray it with cooking spray. 2. Beat the eggs with the water in a shallow bowl until combined. Add the milk, melted butter, bourbon, and vanilla and stir to mix well. 3. Dredge 4 slices of bread in the batter, turning to coat both sides evenly. Transfer the bread slices onto the parchment paper. 4. Bake for 6 minutes until nicely browned. Flip the slices halfway through the cooking time. 5. Remove from the basket to a plate and repeat with the remaining 4 slices of bread. 6. Serve warm.

Blueberry Cobbler

Prep time: 5 minutes | Cook time: 15 minutes | Serves 4

40 g wholemeal pastry flour

¾ teaspoon baking powder

Dash sea salt

120 ml semi-skimmed milk

2 tablespoons pure maple syrup

½ teaspoon vanilla extract

Cooking oil spray

120 g fresh blueberries

60 g muesli

1. In a medium bowl, whisk the flour, baking powder, and salt. Add the milk, maple syrup, and vanilla and gently whisk, just until thoroughly combined. 2. Preheat the unit by selecting BAKE, setting the temperature to 180ºC, and setting the time to 3 minutes. Select START/STOP to begin. 3. Spray a 6-by-2-inch round baking pan with cooking oil and pour the batter into the pan. Top evenly with the blueberries and muesli. 4. Once the unit is preheated, place the pan into the basket. 5. Select BAKE, set the temperature to 180º C, and set the time to 15 minutes. Select START/STOP to begin. 6. When the cooking is complete, the cobbler should be nicely browned and a knife inserted into the middle should come out clean. Enjoy plain or topped with a little vanilla yoghurt.

Jalapeño Popper Egg Cups

Prep time: 10 minutes | Cook time: 10 minutes | Serves 2

4 large eggs

60 g chopped pickled jalapeños

60 g full-fat soft cheese

120 g grated mature Cheddar cheese

1. In a medium bowl, beat the eggs, then pour into four silicone muffin cups. 2. In a large microwave-safe bowl, place jalapeños, soft cheese, and Cheddar. Microwave for 30 seconds and stir. Take a spoonful, approximately ¼ of the mixture, and place it in the

center of one of the egg cups. Repeat with remaining mixture. 3. Place egg cups into the air fryer basket. 4. Adjust the temperature to 160 º C and bake for 10 minutes. 5. Serve warm.

Denver Omelette

Prep time: 5 minutes | Cook time: 8 minutes | Serves 1

2 large eggs

60 ml unsweetened, unflavoured almond milk

¼ teaspoon fine sea salt

⅛ teaspoon ground black pepper

60 g diced gammon (omit for vegetarian)

60 g diced green and red peppers

2 tablespoons diced spring onions, plus more for garnish

60 g grated Cheddar cheese (about 30 g) (omit for dairy-free)

Quartered cherry tomatoes, for serving (optional)

1. Preheat the air fryer to 180ºC. Grease a cake pan and set aside. 2. In a small bowl, use a fork to whisk together the eggs, almond milk, salt, and pepper. Add the gammon, peppers, and spring onions. Pour the mixture into the greased pan. Add the cheese on top (if using). 3. Place the pan in the basket of the air fryer. Bake for 8 minutes, or until the eggs are cooked to your liking. 4. Loosen the omelette from the sides of the pan with a spatula and place it on a serving plate. Garnish with spring onions and serve with cherry tomatoes, if desired. Best served fresh.

Cheddar Eggs

Prep time: 5 minutes | Cook time: 15 minutes | Serves 2

4 large eggs

2 tablespoons unsalted butter, melted

120 g grated mature Cheddar cheese

1. Crack eggs into a round baking dish and whisk. Place dish into the air fryer basket. 2. Adjust the temperature to 200ºC and set the timer for 10 minutes. 3. After 5 minutes, stir the eggs and add the butter and cheese. Let cook 3 more minutes and stir again. 4. Allow eggs to finish cooking an additional 2 minutes or remove if they are to your desired liking. 5. Use a fork to fluff. Serve warm.

Chapter 2 Family Favorites

Meatball Subs

Prep time: 15 minutes | Cook time: 19 minutes | Serves 6

Oil, for spraying

450 g 15% fat minced beef

120 ml Italian breadcrumbs (mixed breadcrumbs, Italian seasoning and salt)

1 tablespoon dried minced onion

1 tablespoon minced garlic

1 large egg

1 teaspoon salt

1 teaspoon freshly ground black pepper

6 sub rolls

1 (510 g) jar marinara sauce

350 ml shredded Mozzarella cheese

1. Line the air fryer basket with parchment and spray lightly with oil. 2. In a large bowl, mix together the ground beef, bread crumbs, onion, garlic, egg, salt, and black pepper. Roll the mixture into 18 meatballs. 3. Place the meatballs in the prepared basket. 4. Air fry at 390°F (199°C) for 15 minutes. 5. Place 3 meatballs in each hoagie roll. Top with marinara and Mozzarella cheese. 6. Place the loaded rolls in the air fryer and cook for 3 to 4 minutes, or until the cheese is melted. You may need to work in batches, depending on the size of your air fryer. Serve immediately.

Apple Pie Egg Rolls

Prep time: 10 minutes | Cook time: 8 minutes | Makes 6 rolls

Oil, for spraying

1 (600 g) tin apple pie filling

1 tablespoon plain flour

½ teaspoon lemon juice

¼ teaspoon ground nutmeg

¼ teaspoon ground cinnamon

6 egg roll wrappers

1. Preheat the air fryer to 200°C. 2.Line the air fryer basket with parchment and spray lightly with oil. 3.In a medium bowl, mix together the pie filling, flour, lemon juice, nutmeg, and cinnamon. 4.Lay out the egg roll wrappers on a work surface and spoon a dollop of pie filling in the centre of each. 5.Fill a small bowl with water. Dip your finger in the water and, working one at a time, moisten the edges of the wrappers. 6.Fold the wrapper like an packet: First fold one corner into the centre. 7.Fold each side corner in, and then fold over the remaining corner, making sure each corner overlaps a bit and the moistened edges stay closed. 8.Use additional water and your fingers to seal any open edges. 9.Place the rolls in the prepared basket and spray liberally with oil. 10.You may need to work in batches, depending on the size of your air fryer. 11.Cook for 4 minutes, flip, spray with oil, and cook for another 4 minutes, or until crispy and golden brown. 12.Serve immediately.

Old Bay Tilapia

Prep time: 15 minutes | Cook time: 6 minutes | Serves 4

Oil, for spraying

235 ml panko breadcrumbs

2 tablespoons Old Bay or all-purpose seasoning

2 teaspoons granulated garlic

1 teaspoon onion powder

½ teaspoon salt

¼ teaspoon freshly ground black pepper

1 large egg

4 tilapia fillets

1. Preheat the air fryer to 204°C. Line the air fryer basket with parchment and spray lightly with oil. 2. In a shallow bowl, mix together the breadcrumbs, seasoning, garlic, onion powder, salt, and black pepper. 3. In a small bowl, whisk the egg. Coat the tilapia in the egg, then dredge in the bread crumb mixture until completely coated. 4. Place the tilapia in the prepared basket. You may need to work in batches, depending on the size of your air fryer. 5. Spray lightly with oil. Cook for 4 to 6 minutes, depending on the thickness of the fillets, until the internal temperature reaches 64°C. 6. Serve immediately.

Fish and Vegetable Tacos

Prep time: 15 minutes | Cook time: 9 to 12 minutes | Serves 4

450 g white fish fillets, such as sole or cod

2 teaspoons olive oil

3 tablespoons freshly squeezed lemon juice, divided

350 g chopped red cabbage

1 large carrot, grated

120 ml low-salt salsa

80 ml low-fat Greek yoghurt

4 soft low-salt wholemeal maize wraps

1. Brush the fish with the olive oil and sprinkle with 1 tablespoon of lemon juice. 2. Air fry in the air fryer basket at 200°C for 9 to 12 minutes, or until the fish just flakes when tested with a fork. 3. Meanwhile, in a medium bowl, stir together the remaining 2 tablespoons of lemon juice, the red cabbage, carrot, salsa, and yoghurt. 4. When the fish is cooked, remove it from the air fryer basket and break it up into large pieces. 5. Offer the fish, maize wraps, and the cabbage mixture, and let each person assemble a taco.

Steak and Vegetable Kebabs

Prep time: 15 minutes | Cook time: 5 to 7 minutes | Serves 4

2 tablespoons balsamic vinegar

2 teaspoons olive oil

½ teaspoon dried marjoram

⅛ teaspoon ground black pepper

340 g silverside, cut into 1-inch pieces

1 red pepper, sliced

16 button mushrooms

235 g cherry tomatoes

1. In a medium bowl, stir together the balsamic vinegar, olive oil, marjoram, and black pepper. 2. Add the steak and stir to coat. Let stand for 10 minutes at room temperature. 3. Alternating items, thread the beef, red pepper, mushrooms, and tomatoes onto 8 bamboo or metal skewers that fit in the air fryer. 4. Air fry at 200°C for 5 to 7 minutes, or until the beef is browned and reaches at least 64°C on a meat thermometer. 5. Serve immediately.

Mushroom and Green Bean Casserole

Prep time: 10 minutes | Cook time: 15 minutes | Serves 4

4 tablespoons unsalted butter

60 g diced brown onion

120 g chopped white mushrooms

120 ml double cream

30 g full fat soft white cheese

120 g chicken broth

¼ teaspoon xanthan gum

450 g fresh green beans, edges trimmed

14 g pork crackling, finely ground

1. In a medium skillet over medium heat, melt the butter 2.Sauté the onion and mushrooms until they become soft and fragrant, about 3 to 5 minutes 3.Add the double cream, soft white cheese, and broth to the pan 4.Whisk until smooth 5.Bring to a boil and then reduce to a simmer 6.Sprinkle the xanthan gum into the pan and remove from heat 7.Preheat the air fryer to 160°C 8.Chop the green beans into 2-inch pieces and place into a baking dish 9.Pour the sauce mixture over them and stir until coated 10.Top the dish with minced pork crackling 11.Put into the air fryer basket and bake for 15 minutes 12.Top will be golden and green beans fork-tender when fully cooked 13.Serve warm.

Chinese-Inspired Spareribs

Prep time: 30 minutes | Cook time: 8 minutes | Serves 4

Oil, for spraying

340 g pork ribs, cut into 3-inch-long pieces

235 ml soy sauce

140 g sugar

120 g beef broth

60 ml honey

2 tablespoons minced garlic

1 teaspoon ground ginger

2 drops red food dye (optional)

1. Line the air fryer basket with parchment and spray lightly with oil. 2.Combine the ribs, soy sauce, sugar, beef broth, honey, garlic, ginger, and food colouring (if using) in a large zip-top plastic bag, seal, and shake well until completely coated. 3.Refrigerate for at least 30 minutes. 4.Place the ribs in the prepared basket. 5.Air fry at 190°C for 8 minutes, or until the internal temperature reaches 74°C.

Personal Cauliflower Pizzas

Prep time: 10 minutes | Cook time: 25 minutes | Serves 2

1 (340 g) bag frozen riced cauliflower

75 g shredded Mozzarella cheese

15 g almond flour

20 g Parmesan cheese

1 large egg

½ teaspoon salt

1 teaspoon garlic powder

1 teaspoon dried oregano

4 tablespoons no-sugar-added marinara sauce, divided

110 g fresh Mozzarella, chopped, divided

140 g cooked chicken breast, chopped, divided

100 g chopped cherry tomatoes, divided

5 g fresh baby rocket, divided

1. Preheat the air fryer to 200°C. Cut 4 sheets of parchment paper to fit the basket of the air fryer. Brush with olive oil and set aside. 2. In a large glass bowl, microwave the cauliflower according to package directions. Place the cauliflower on a clean towel, draw up the sides, and squeeze tightly over a sink to remove the excess moisture. Return the cauliflower to the bowl and add the shredded Mozzarella along with the almond flour, Parmesan, egg, salt, garlic powder, and oregano. Stir until thoroughly combined. 3. Divide the dough into two equal portions. Place one piece of dough on the prepared parchment paper and pat gently into a thin, flat disk 7 to 8 inches in diameter. Air fry for 15 minutes until the crust begins to brown. Let cool for 5 minutes. 4. Transfer the parchment paper with the crust on top to a baking sheet. Place a second sheet of parchment paper over the crust. While holding the edges of both sheets together, carefully lift the crust off

the baking sheet, flip it, and place it back in the air fryer basket. The new sheet of parchment paper is now on the bottom. Remove the top piece of paper and air fry the crust for another 15 minutes until the top begins to brown. Remove the basket from the air fryer. 5. Spread 2 tablespoons of the marinara sauce on top of the crust, followed by half the fresh Mozzarella, chicken, cherry tomatoes, and rocket. Air fry for 5 to 10 minutes longer, until the cheese is melted and beginning to brown. Remove the pizza from the oven and let it sit for 10 minutes before serving. Repeat with the remaining ingredients to make a second pizza.

Berry Cheesecake

Prep time: 5 minutes | Cook time: 10 minutes | Serves 4

Oil, for spraying

227 g soft white cheese

6 tablespoons sugar

1 tablespoon sour cream

1 large egg

½ teaspoon vanilla extract

¼ teaspoon lemon juice

120 g fresh mixed berries

1. Preheat the air fryer to 180°C. 2.Line the air fryer basket with parchment and spray lightly with oil. 3.In a blender, combine the soft white cheese, sugar, sour cream, egg, vanilla, and lemon juice and blend until smooth. 4.Pour the mixture into a 4-inch springform pan. 5.Place the pan in the prepared basket. Cook for 8

to 10 minutes, or until only the very centre jiggles slightly when the pan is moved. 6.Refrigerate the cheesecake in the pan for at least 2 hours. 7.Release the sides from the springform pan, top the cheesecake with the mixed berries, and serve.

Fried Green Tomatoes

Prep time: 15 minutes | Cook time: 6 to 8 minutes | Serves 4

4 medium green tomatoes

50 g plain flour

2 egg whites

60 ml almond milk

235 g ground almonds

120 g Japanese breadcrumbs

2 teaspoons olive oil

1 teaspoon paprika

1 clove garlic, minced

1. Rinse the tomatoes and pat dry. 2.Cut the tomatoes into ½-inch slices, discarding the thinner ends. Put the flour on a plate. 3.In a shallow bowl, beat the egg whites with the almond milk until frothy. 4.And on another plate, combine the almonds, breadcrumbs, olive oil, paprika, and garlic and mix well. 5.Dip the tomato slices into the flour, then into the egg white mixture, then into the almond mixture to coat. 6.Place four of the coated tomato slices in the air fryer basket. 7.Air fry at 200ºC for 6 to 8 minutes or until the tomato coating is crisp and golden brown. 8.Repeat with remaining tomato slices and serve immediately.

Chapter 3 Fast and Easy Everyday Favourites

Easy Devils on Horseback

Prep time: 5 minutes | Cook time: 7 minutes | Serves 12

24 small pitted prunes (128 g)

60 g crumbled blue cheese, divided

8 slices middle bacon, cut crosswise into thirds

1. Preheat the air fryer to 200°C. 2.Halve the prunes lengthwise, but don't cut them all the way through. 3.Place ½ teaspoon of cheese in the centre of each prune. 4.Wrap a piece of bacon around each prune and secure the bacon with a toothpick. 5.Working in batches, arrange a single layer of the prunes in the air fryer basket. 6.Air fry for about 7 minutes, flipping halfway, until the bacon is cooked through and crisp. 7.Let cool slightly and serve warm.

Simple and Easy Croutons

Prep time: 5 minutes | Cook time: 8 minutes | Serves 4

2 sliced bread

1 tablespoon olive oil

Hot soup, for serving

1. Preheat the air fryer to 200°C. 2.Cut the slices of bread into medium-size chunks. 3.Brush the air fryer basket with the oil. 4.Place the chunks inside and air fry for at least 8 minutes. 5.Serve with hot soup.

Southwest Corn and Pepper Roast

Prep time: 10 minutes | Cook time: 10 minutes | Serves 4

For the Corn:

350 g thawed frozen corn kernels

235 g mixed diced peppers

1 jalapeño, diced

235 g diced brown onion

½ teaspoon ancho chilli powder

1 tablespoon fresh lemon juice

1 teaspoon ground cumin

½ teaspoon rock salt

Cooking spray

For Serving:

60 g feta cheese

60 g chopped fresh coriander

1 tablespoon fresh lemon juice

1. Preheat the air fryer to 190°C 2.Spritz the air fryer with cooking spray 3.Combine the ingredients for the corn in a large bowl 4.Stir to mix well 5.Pour the mixture into the air fryer 6.Air fry for 10 minutes or until the corn and peppers are soft 7.Shake the basket halfway through the cooking time 8.Transfer them onto a large plate, then spread with feta cheese and coriander 9.Drizzle with lemon juice and serve.

Baked Cheese Sandwich

Prep time: 5 minutes | Cook time: 8 minutes | Serves 2

2 tablespoons mayonnaise

4 thick slices sourdough bread

4 thick slices Brie cheese

8 slices hot capicola or prosciutto

1. Preheat the air fryer to 180 °C. 2.Spread the mayonnaise on one side of each slice of bread. 3.Place

2 slices of bread in the air fryer basket, mayonnaise-side down. 4.Place the slices of Brie and capicola on the bread and cover with the remaining two slices of bread, mayonnaise-side up. 5.Bake for 8 minutes, or until the cheese has melted. 6.Serve immediately.

Herb-Roasted Veggies

Prep time: 10 minutes | Cook time: 14 to 18 minutes | Serves 4

1 red pepper, sliced

1 (230 g) package sliced mushrooms

235 g runner beans, cut into 2-inch pieces

80 g diced red onion

3 garlic cloves, sliced

1 teaspoon olive oil

½ teaspoon dried basil

½ teaspoon dried tarragon

1. Preheat the air fryer to 180°C. 2.In a medium bowl, mix the red pepper, mushrooms, runner beans, red onion, and garlic. 3.Drizzle with the olive oil. Toss to coat. 4.Add the herbs and toss again. Place the vegetables in the air fryer basket. 5.Roast for 14 to 18 minutes, or until tender. 6.Serve immediately.

Air Fried Courgette Sticks

Prep time: 5 minutes | Cook time: 20 minutes | Serves 4

1 medium courgette, cut into 48 sticks

30 g seasoned breadcrumbs

1 tablespoon melted margarine

Cooking spray

1. Preheat the air fryer to 180°C. Spritz the air fryer basket with cooking spray and set aside. In 2 different shallow bowls, add the seasoned breadcrumbs and the margarine. One by one, dredge the courgette sticks into

the margarine, then roll in the breadcrumbs to coat evenly. Arrange the crusted sticks on a plate. Place the courgette sticks in the prepared air fryer basket. Work in two batches to avoid overcrowding. Air fry for 10 minutes, or until golden brown and crispy. Shake the basket halfway through to cook evenly. When the cooking time is over, transfer the fries to a wire rack. Rest for 5 minutes and serve warm.

Baked Chorizo Scotch Eggs

Prep time:5 minutes | Cook time: 15 to 20 minutes | Makes 4 eggs

450 g Mexican chorizo or other seasoned banger meat

4 soft-boiled eggs plus 1 raw egg

1 tablespoon water

120 ml plain flour

235 ml panko breadcrumbs

Cooking spray

1. Divide the chorizo into 4 equal portions. Flatten each portion into a disc. Place a soft-boiled egg in the centre of each disc. Wrap the chorizo around the egg, encasing it completely. Place the encased eggs on a plate and chill for at least 30 minutes. 2.Preheat the air fryer to 182°C. 3.Beat the raw egg with 1 tablespoon of water. Place the flour on a small plate and the panko on a second plate. Working with 1 egg at a time, roll the encased egg in the flour, then dip it in the egg mixture. Dredge the egg in the panko and place on a plate. Repeat with the remaining eggs. 4.Spray the eggs with oil and place in the air fryer basket. Bake for 10 minutes. Turn and bake for an additional 5 to 10 minutes, or until browned and crisp on all sides. 5.Serve immediately.

Sweet Maize and Carrot Fritters

Prep time: 10 minutes | Cook time: 8 to 11 minutes | Serves 4

1 medium-sized carrot, grated

1 brown onion, finely chopped

4 ounces (113 g) canned sweet maize kernels, drained

1 teaspoon sea salt flakes

1 tablespoon chopped fresh coriander

1 medium-sized egg, whisked

2 tablespoons plain milk

1 cup grated Parmesan cheese

¼ cup flour

⅓ teaspoon baking powder

⅓ teaspoon sugar

Cooking spray

1. Preheat the air fryer to 350°F (177°C). 2. Place the grated carrot in a colander and press down to squeeze out any excess moisture. Dry it with a paper towel. 3. Combine the carrots with the remaining ingredients. 4. Mold 1 tablespoon of the mixture into a ball and press it down with your hand or a spoon to flatten it. Repeat until the rest of the mixture is used up. 5. Spritz the balls with cooking spray. 6. Arrange in the air fryer basket, taking care not to overlap any balls. Bake for 8 to 11 minutes, or until they're firm. 7. Serve warm.

Air Fried Shishito Peppers

Prep time: 5 minutes | Cook time: 5 minutes | Serves 4

230 g shishito or Padron peppers (about 24)

1 tablespoon olive oil

Coarse sea salt, to taste

Lemon wedges, for serving

Cooking spray

1. Preheat the air fryer to 200°C. 2.Spritz the air fryer basket with cooking spray. 3.Toss the peppers with olive oil in a large bowl to coat well. Arrange the peppers in the preheated air fryer. 4.Air fryer for 5 minutes or until blistered and lightly charred. Shake the basket and sprinkle the peppers with salt halfway through the cooking time. 5.Transfer the peppers onto a plate and squeeze the lemon wedges on top before serving.

Cheesy Baked Coarse Cornmeal

Prep time: 10 minutes | Cook time: 12 minutes | Serves 6

180 ml hot water

2 (28 g) packages instant grits

1 large egg, beaten

1 tablespoon melted butter

2 cloves garlic, minced

½ to 1 teaspoon red pepper flakes

235 g shredded Cheddar cheese or jalapeño Jack cheese

1. Preheat the air fryer to 200°C. 2.In a baking tray, combine the water, coarse cornmeal, egg, butter, garlic, and red pepper flakes. Stir until well combined. 3.Stir in the shredded cheese. 4.Place the pan in the air fryer basket and air fry for 12 minutes, or until the coarse cornmeal have cooked through and a knife inserted near the centre comes out clean. 5.Let stand for 5 minutes before serving.

Chapter 4 Poultry

Broccoli Cheese Chicken

Prep time: 15 minutes | Cook time: 25 minutes | Serves 4

1 tablespoon avocado oil

15 g chopped onion

35 g finely chopped broccoli

115 g cream cheese, at room temperature

60 g Cheddar cheese, shredded

1 teaspoon garlic powder

½ teaspoon sea salt, plus additional for seasoning, divided

¼ freshly ground black pepper, plus additional for seasoning, divided

900 g boneless, skinless chicken breasts

1 teaspoon smoked paprika

1. Heat a medium frying pan over medium-high heat and pour in the avocado oil. Add the onion and broccoli and cook, stirring occasionally, for 5 to 8 minutes, until the onion is tender. 2. Transfer to a large bowl and stir in the cream cheese, Cheddar cheese, and garlic powder, and season to taste with salt and pepper. 3. Hold a sharp knife parallel to the chicken breast and cut a long pocket into one side. Stuff the chicken pockets with the broccoli mixture, using toothpicks to secure the pockets around the filling. 4. In a small dish, combine the paprika, ½ teaspoon salt, and ¼ teaspoon pepper. Sprinkle this over the outside of the chicken. 5. Set the air fryer to 200ºC. Place the chicken in a single layer in the air fryer basket, cooking in batches if necessary, and cook for 14 to 16 minutes, until an instant-read thermometer reads 70ºC. Place the chicken on a plate and tent a piece of aluminium foil over the chicken. Allow to rest for 5 to 10 minutes before serving.

Easy Chicken Nachos

Prep time: 5 minutes | Cook time: 5 minutes | Serves 8

Oil, for spraying

420 g shredded cooked chicken

1 (30 g) package ranch seasoning

60 g sour cream

55 g maize wraps chips

75 g bacon bits

235 g shredded Cheddar cheese

1 tablespoon chopped spring onions

1. Line the air fryer basket with parchment and spray lightly with oil. 2. In a small bowl, mix together the chicken, ranch seasoning, and sour cream. 3. Place the maize wraps crisps in the prepared basket and top with the chicken mixture. Add the bacon bits, Cheddar cheese, and spring onions. 4. Air fry at 220ºC for 3 to 5 minutes, or until heated through and the cheese is melted.

Chicken and Avocado Fajitas

Prep time: 10 minutes | Cook time: 10 to 14 minutes | Serves 4

Cooking oil spray

4 boneless, skinless chicken breasts, sliced crosswise

1 small red onion, sliced

2 red peppers, seeded and sliced

120 ml spicy ranch salad dressing, divided

½ teaspoon dried oregano

8 maize wraps

40 g torn butter lettuce leaves

2 avocados, peeled, pitted, and chopped

1. Insert the crisper plate into the basket and the basket into the unit. Preheat the unit by selecting BAKE, setting the temperature to 190°C, and setting the time to 3 minutes. Select START/STOP to begin. 2. Once the unit is preheated, spray the crisper plate with cooking oil. Place the chicken, red onion, and red pepper into the basket. Drizzle with 1 tablespoon of the salad dressing and season with the oregano. Toss to combine. 3. Select BAKE, set the temperature to 190°C, and set the time to 14 minutes. Select START/STOP to begin. 4. After 10 minutes, check the chicken. If a food thermometer inserted into the chicken registers at least 76°C, it is done. If not, resume cooking. 5. When the cooking is complete, transfer the chicken and vegetables to a bowl and toss with the remaining salad dressing. 6. Serve the chicken mixture family-style with the corn wraps, lettuce, and avocados, and let everyone make their own plates.

Chicken Shawarma

Prep time: 30 minutes | Cook time: 15 minutes | Serves 4

Shawarma Spice:

2 teaspoons dried oregano

1 teaspoon ground cinnamon

1 teaspoon ground cumin

1 teaspoon ground coriander

1 teaspoon kosher salt

½ teaspoon ground allspice

½ teaspoon cayenne pepper

Chicken:

450 g boneless, skinless chicken thighs, cut into large bite-size chunks

2 tablespoons vegetable oil

For Serving:

Tzatziki

Pita bread

1. For the shawarma spice: In a small bowl, combine the oregano, cayenne, cumin, coriander, salt, cinnamon, and allspice. 2. For the chicken: In a large bowl, toss together the chicken, vegetable oil, and shawarma spice to coat. Marinate at room temperature for 30 minutes or cover and refrigerate for up to 24 hours. 3. Place the chicken in the air fryer basket. Set the air fryer to 180°C for 15 minutes, or until the chicken reaches an internal temperature of 76°C. 4. Transfer the chicken to a serving platter. Serve with tzatziki and pita bread.

Chicken Burgers with Gammon and Cheese

Prep time: 12 minutes | Cook time: 13 to 16 minutes | Serves 4

20 g soft bread crumbs

3 tablespoons milk

1 egg, beaten

½ teaspoon dried thyme

Pinch salt

Freshly ground black pepper, to taste

570 g chicken mince

70 g finely choppedgammon

75 g grated Gouda cheese

Olive oil for misting

1. Preheat the air fryer to 180°C. 2. In a medium bowl, combine the bread crumbs, milk, egg, thyme, salt, and pepper. Add the chicken and mix gently but thoroughly with clean hands. 3. Form the chicken into eight thin patties and place on waxed paper. 4. Top four of the patties with the gammon and cheese. Top with remaining four patties and gently press the edges together to seal, so the gammon and cheese mixture is

in the middle of the burger. 5. Place the burgers in the basket and mist with olive oil. Bake for 13 to 16 minutes or until the chicken is thoroughly cooked to 76 º C as measured with a meat thermometer. Serve immediately.

Classic Whole Chicken

Prep time: 5 minutes | Cook time: 50 minutes | Serves 4

Oil, for spraying

1 (1.8 kg) whole chicken, giblets removed

1 tablespoon olive oil

1 teaspoon paprika

½ teaspoon granulated garlic

½ teaspoon salt

½ teaspoon freshly ground black pepper

¼ teaspoon finely chopped fresh parsley, for garnish

1. Line the air fryer basket with parchment and spray lightly with oil. 2. Pat the chicken dry with paper towels. Rub it with the olive oil until evenly coated. 3. In a small bowl, mix together the paprika, garlic, salt, and black pepper and sprinkle it evenly over the chicken. 4. Place the chicken in the prepared basket, breast-side down. 5. Air fry at 180°C for 30 minutes, flip, and cook for another 20 minutes, or until the internal temperature reaches 76°C and the juices run clear. 6. Sprinkle with the parsley before serving.

Chicken and Broccoli Casserole

Prep time: 5 minutes | Cook time: 20 to 25 minutes | Serves 4

230 g broccoli, chopped into florets

280 g shredded cooked chicken

115 g cream cheese

80 g double cream

1½ teaspoons Dijon mustard

½ teaspoon garlic powder

Salt and freshly ground black pepper, to taste

2 tablespoons chopped fresh basil

230 g shredded Cheddar cheese

1. Preheat the air fryer to 200 º C. Lightly coat a casserole dish that will fit in air fryer, with olive oil and set aside. 2. Place the broccoli in a large glass bowl with 1 tablespoon of water and cover with a microwavable plate. Microwave on high for 2 to 3 minutes until the broccoli is bright green but not mushy. Drain if necessary and add to another large bowl along with the shredded chicken. 3. In the same glass bowl used to microwave the broccoli, combine the cream cheese and cream. Microwave for 30 seconds to 1 minute on high and stir until smooth. Add the mustard and garlic powder and season to taste with salt and freshly ground black pepper. Whisk until the sauce is smooth. 4. Pour the warm sauce over the broccoli and chicken mixture and then add the basil. Using a silicone spatula, gently fold the mixture until thoroughly combined. 5. Transfer the chicken mixture to the prepared casserole dish and top with the cheese. Air fry for 20 to 25 minutes until warmed through and the cheese has browned.

Coconut Chicken Meatballs

Prep time: 10 minutes | Cook time: 14 minutes | Serves 4

450 g chicken mince

2 spring onions, finely chopped

20 g chopped fresh corinader leaves

20 g unsweetened desiccated coconut

1 tablespoon hoisin sauce

1 tablespoon soy sauce

2 teaspoons Sriracha or other hot sauce

1 teaspoon toasted sesame oil

½ teaspoon kosher salt

1 teaspoon black pepper

1. In a large bowl, gently mix the chicken, spring onions, coriander, coconut, hoisin, soy sauce, Sriracha, sesame oil, salt, and pepper until thoroughly combined (the mixture will be wet and sticky). 2. Place a sheet of parchment paper in the air fryer basket. Using a small scoop or teaspoon, drop rounds of the mixture in a single layer onto the parchment paper. 3. Set the air fryer to 180°C for 10 minutes, turning the meatballs halfway through the cooking time. Raise the air fryer temperature to 200°C and cook for 4 minutes more to brown the outsides of the meatballs. Use a meat thermometer to ensure the meatballs have reached an internal temperature of 76ºC. 4. Transfer the meatballs to a serving platter. Repeat with any remaining chicken mixture.

Blackened Chicken

Prep time: 10 minutes | Cook time: 20 minutes | Serves 4

1 large egg, beaten

215 g Blackened seasoning

2 whole boneless, skinless chicken breasts (about 450 g each), halved

1 to 2 tablespoons oil

1. Place the beaten egg in one shallow bowl and the Blackened seasoning in another shallow bowl. 2. One at a time, dip the chicken pieces in the beaten egg and the Blackened seasoning, coating thoroughly. 3. Preheat the air fryer to 180ºC. Line the air fryer basket with parchment paper. 4. Place the chicken pieces on the parchment and spritz with oil. 5. Cook for 10 minutes. Flip the chicken, spritz it with oil, and cook for 10 minutes more until the internal temperature reaches 76ºC and the chicken is no longer pink inside. Let sit for 5 minutes before serving.

Sriracha-Honey Chicken Nuggets

Prep time: 15 minutes | Cook time: 19 minutes | Serves 6

Oil, for spraying

1 large egg

180 ml milk

65 g plain flour

2 tablespoons icing sugar

½ teaspoon paprika

½ teaspoon salt

½ teaspoon freshly ground black pepper

2 boneless, skinless chicken breasts, cut into bite-size pieces

140 g barbecue sauce

2 tablespoons honey

1 tablespoon Sriracha

1. Line the air fryer basket with parchment and spray lightly with oil. 2. In a small bowl, whisk together the egg and milk. 3. In a medium bowl, combine the flour, icing sugar, paprika, salt, and black pepper and stir. 4. Coat the chicken in the egg mixture, then dredge in the flour mixture until evenly coated. 5. Place the chicken in the prepared basket and spray liberally with oil. 6. Air fry at 200ºC for 8 minutes, flip, spray with more oil, and cook for another 6 to 8 minutes, or until the internal temperature reaches 76°C and the juices run clear. 7. In a large bowl, mix together the barbecue sauce, honey, and Sriracha. 8. Transfer the chicken to the bowl and toss until well coated with the barbecue sauce mixture. 9. Line the air fryer basket with fresh parchment, return the chicken to the basket, and cook for another 2 to 3 minutes, until browned and crispy.

Sweet Chili Spiced Chicken

Prep time: 10 minutes | Cook time: 43

minutes | Serves 4

Spice Rub:

2 tablespoons brown sugar

2 tablespoons paprika

1 teaspoon dry mustard powder

1 teaspoon chilli powder

2 tablespoons coarse sea salt or kosher salt

2 teaspoons coarsely ground black pepper

1 tablespoon vegetable oil

1 (1.6 kg) chicken, cut into 8 pieces

1. Prepare the spice rub by combining the brown sugar, paprika, mustard powder, chilli powder, salt and pepper. Rub the oil all over the chicken pieces and then rub the spice mix onto the chicken, covering completely. This is done very easily in a zipper sealable bag. You tin do this ahead of time and let the chicken marinate in the refrigerator, or just proceed with cooking right away. 2. Preheat the air fryer to 190°C. 3. Air fry the chicken in two batches. Place the two chicken thighs and two drumsticks into the air fryer basket. Air fry at 190°C for 10 minutes. Then, gently turn the chicken pieces over and air fry for another 10 minutes. Remove the chicken pieces and let them rest on a plate while you cook the chicken breasts. Air fry the chicken breasts, skin side down for 8 minutes. Turn the chicken breasts over and air fry for another 12 minutes. 4. Lower the temperature of the air fryer to 170°C. Place the first batch of chicken on top of the second batch already in the basket and air fry for a final 3 minutes. 5. Let the chicken rest for 5 minutes and serve warm with some mashed potatoes and a green salad or vegetables.

Butter and Bacon Chicken

Prep time: 10 minutes | Cook time: 65 minutes | Serves 6

1 (1.8 kg) whole chicken

2 tablespoons salted butter, softened

1 teaspoon dried thyme

½ teaspoon garlic powder

1 teaspoon salt

½ teaspoon ground black pepper

6 slices sugar-free bacon

1. Pat chicken dry with a paper towel, then rub with butter on all sides. Sprinkle thyme, garlic powder, salt, and pepper over chicken. 2. Place chicken into ungreased air fryer basket, breast side up. Lay strips of bacon over chicken and secure with toothpicks. 3. Adjust the temperature to 180°C and air fry for 65 minutes. Halfway through cooking, remove and set aside bacon and flip chicken over. Chicken will be done when the skin is golden and crispy and the internal temperature is at least 76°C. Serve warm with bacon.

Pomegranate-Glazed Chicken with Couscous Salad

Prep time: 25 minutes | Cook time: 20 minutes | Serves 4

3 tablespoons plus 2 teaspoons pomegranate black treacle

½ teaspoon ground cinnamon

1 teaspoon minced fresh thyme

Salt and ground black pepper, to taste

2 (340 g) bone-in split chicken breasts, trimmed

60 ml chicken broth

60 ml water

80 g couscous

1 tablespoon minced fresh parsley

60 g cherry tomatoes, quartered

1 scallion, white part minced, green part sliced thin

on bias

1 tablespoon extra-virgin olive oil

30 g feta cheese, crumbled

Cooking spray

1. Preheat the air fryer to 180°C. Spritz the air fryer basket with cooking spray. 2. Combine 3 tablespoons of pomegranate black treacle, cinnamon, thyme, and ⅛ teaspoon of salt in a small bowl. Stir to mix well. Set aside. 3. Place the chicken breasts in the preheated air fryer, skin side down, and spritz with cooking spray. Sprinkle with salt and ground black pepper. 4. Air fry the chicken for 10 minutes, then brush the chicken with half of pomegranate black treacle mixture and flip. Air fry for 5 more minutes. 5. Brush the chicken with remaining pomegranate black treacle mixture and flip. Air fry for another 5 minutes or until the internal temperature of the chicken breasts reaches at least 76° C. 6. Meanwhile, pour the broth and water in a pot and bring to a boil over medium-high heat. Add the couscous and sprinkle with salt. Cover and simmer for 7 minutes or until the liquid is almost absorbed. 7. Combine the remaining ingredients, except for the cheese, with cooked couscous in a large bowl. Toss to mix well. Scatter with the feta cheese. 8. When the air frying is complete, remove the chicken from the air fryer and allow to cool for 10 minutes. Serve with vegetable and couscous salad.

Nashville Hot Chicken

Prep time: 20 minutes | Cook time: 24 to 28 minutes | Serves 8

1.4 kg bone-in, skin-on chicken pieces, breasts halved crosswise

1 tablespoon sea salt

1 tablespoon freshly ground black pepper

70 g finely ground blanched almond flour

130 g grated Parmesan cheese

1 tablespoon baking powder

2 teaspoons garlic powder, divided

120 g heavy (whipping) cream

2 large eggs, beaten

1 tablespoon vinegar-based hot sauce

Avocado oil spray

115 g unsalted butter

120 ml avocado oil

1 tablespoon cayenne pepper (more or less to taste)

2 tablespoons Xylitol

1. Sprinkle the chicken with the salt and pepper. 2. In a large shallow bowl, whisk together the almond flour, Parmesan cheese, baking powder, and 1 teaspoon of the garlic powder. 3. In a separate bowl, whisk together the double cream, eggs, and hot sauce. 4. Dip the chicken pieces in the egg, then coat each with the almond flour mixture, pressing the mixture into the chicken to adhere. Allow to sit for 15 minutes to let the breading set. 5. Set the air fryer to 200°C. Place the chicken in a single layer in the air fryer basket, being careful not to overcrowd the pieces, working in batches if necessary. Spray the chicken with oil and roast for 13 minutes. 6. Carefully flip the chicken and spray it with more oil. Reduce the air fryer temperature to 180° C. Roast for another 11 to 15 minutes, until an instant-read thermometer reads 70 °C. 7. While the chicken cooks, heat the butter, avocado oil, cayenne pepper, xylitol, and remaining 1 teaspoon of garlic powder in a saucepan over medium-low heat. Cook until the butter is melted and the sugar substitute has dissolved. 8. Remove the chicken from the air fryer. Use tongs to dip the chicken in the sauce. Place the coated chicken on a rack over a baking sheet, and allow it to rest for 5 minutes before serving.

Piri-Piri Chicken Thighs

Prep time: 5 minutes | Cook time: 25 minutes

| Serves 4

60 ml piri-piri sauce

1 tablespoon freshly squeezed lemon juice

2 tablespoons brown sugar, divided

2 cloves garlic, minced

1 tablespoon extra-virgin olive oil

4 bone-in, skin-on chicken thighs, each weighing approximately 200 to 230 g

½ teaspoon cornflour

1. To make the marinade, whisk together the piri-piri sauce, lemon juice, 1 tablespoon of brown sugar, and the garlic in a small bowl. While whisking, slowly pour in the oil in a steady stream and continue to whisk until emulsified. Using a skewer, poke holes in the chicken thighs and place them in a small glass dish. Pour the marinade over the chicken and turn the thighs to coat them with the sauce. Cover the dish and refrigerate for at least 15 minutes and up to 1 hour. 2. Preheat the air fryer to 190°C. Remove the chicken thighs from the dish, reserving the marinade, and place them skin-side down in the air fryer basket. Air fry until the internal temperature reaches 76°C, 15 to 20 minutes. 3. Meanwhile, whisk the remaining brown sugar and the cornflour into the marinade and microwave it on high power for 1 minute until it is bubbling and thickened to a glaze. 4. Once the chicken is cooked, turn the thighs over and brush them with the glaze. Air fry for a few additional minutes until the glaze browns and begins to char in spots. 5. Remove the chicken to a platter and serve with additional piri-piri sauce, if desired.

Easy Turkey Tenderloin

Prep time: 20 minutes | Cook time: 30 minutes | Serves 4

Olive oil

½ teaspoon paprika

½ teaspoon garlic powder

½ teaspoon salt

½ teaspoon freshly ground black pepper

Pinch cayenne pepper

680 g turkey breast tenderloin

1. Spray the air fryer basket lightly with olive oil. 2. In a small bowl, combine the paprika, garlic powder, salt, black pepper, and cayenne pepper. Rub the mixture all over the turkey. 3. Place the turkey in the air fryer basket and lightly spray with olive oil. 4. Air fry at 190 °C for 15 minutes. Flip the turkey over and lightly spray with olive oil. Air fry until the internal temperature reaches at least 80°C for an additional 10 to 15 minutes. 5. Let the turkey rest for 10 minutes before slicing and serving.

Brazilian Tempero Baiano Chicken Drumsticks

Prep time: 30 minutes | Cook time: 20 minutes | Serves 4

1 teaspoon cumin seeds

1 teaspoon dried oregano

1 teaspoon dried parsley

1 teaspoon ground turmeric

½ teaspoon coriander seeds

1 teaspoon kosher salt

½ teaspoon black peppercorns

½ teaspoon cayenne pepper

60 ml fresh lime juice

2 tablespoons olive oil

680 g chicken drumsticks

1. In a clean coffee grinder or spice mill, combine the cumin, oregano, parsley, turmeric, coriander seeds, salt, peppercorns, and cayenne. Process until finely ground.

2. In a small bowl, combine the ground spices with the lime juice and oil. Place the chicken in a resealable plastic bag. Add the marinade, seal, and massage until the chicken is well coated. Marinate at room temperature for 30 minutes or in the refrigerator for up to 24 hours. 3. When you are ready to cook, place the drumsticks skin side up in the air fryer basket. Set the air fryer to 200ºC for 20 to 25 minutes, turning the legs halfway through the cooking time. Use a meat thermometer to ensure that the chicken has reached an internal temperature of 76ºC. 4. Serve with plenty of serviettes.

Lemon-Basil Turkey Breasts

Prep time: 30 minutes | Cook time: 58 minutes | Serves 4

2 tablespoons olive oil

900 g turkey breasts, bone-in, skin-on

Coarse sea salt and ground black pepper, to taste

1 teaspoon fresh basil leaves, chopped

2 tablespoons lemon zest, grated

1. Rub olive oil on all sides of the turkey breasts; sprinkle with salt, pepper, basil, and lemon zest. 2. Place the turkey breasts skin side up on the parchment-lined air fryer basket. 3. Cook in the preheated air fryer at 170ºC for 30 minutes. Now, turn them over and cook an additional 28 minutes. 4. Serve with lemon wedges, if desired. Bon appétit!

Jalapeño Popper Hasselback Chicken

Prep time: 10 minutes | Cook time: 19 minutes | Serves 2

Oil, for spraying

2 (230 g) boneless, skinless chicken breasts

60 g cream cheese, softened

55 g bacon bits

20 g chopped pickled jalapeños

40 g shredded Cheddar cheese, divided

1. Line the air fryer basket with parchment and spray lightly with oil. 2. Make multiple cuts across the top of each chicken breast, cutting only halfway through. 3. In a medium bowl, mix together the cream cheese, bacon bits, jalapeños, and Cheddar cheese. Spoon some of the mixture into each cut. 4. Place the chicken in the prepared basket. 5. Air fry at 176ºC for 14 minutes. Scatter the remaining cheese on top of the chicken and cook for another 2 to 5 minutes, or until the cheese is melted and the internal temperature reaches 76ºC.

Easy Cajun Chicken Drumsticks

Prep time: 5 minutes | Cook time: 40 minutes | Serves 5

1 tablespoon olive oil

10 chicken drumsticks

1½ tablespoons Cajun seasoning

Salt and ground black pepper, to taste

1. Preheat the air fryer to 200ºC. Grease the air fryer basket with olive oil. 2. On a clean work surface, rub the chicken drumsticks with Cajun seasoning, salt, and ground black pepper. 3. Arrange the seasoned chicken drumsticks in a single layer in the air fryer. You need to work in batches to avoid overcrowding. 4. Air fry for 18 minutes or until lightly browned. Flip the drumsticks halfway through. 5. Remove the chicken drumsticks from the air fryer. Serve immediately.

Buttermilk Breaded Chicken

Prep time: 7 minutes | Cook time: 20 to 25 minutes | Serves 4

125 g plain flour

2 teaspoons paprika

Pinch salt

Freshly ground black pepper, to taste

80 ml buttermilk

2 eggs

2 tablespoons extra-virgin olive oil

185 g bread crumbs

6 chicken pieces, drumsticks, breasts, and thighs, patted dry

Cooking oil spray

1. In a shallow bowl, stir together the flour, paprika, salt, and pepper. 2. In another bowl, beat the buttermilk and eggs until smooth. 3. In a third bowl, stir together the olive oil and bread crumbs until mixed. 4. Dredge the chicken in the flour, dip in the eggs to coat, and finally press into the bread crumbs, patting the crumbs firmly onto the chicken skin. 5. Insert the crisper plate into the basket and the basket into the unit. Preheat the unit by selecting AIR FRY, setting the temperature to 190 ° C, and setting the time to 3 minutes. Select START/STOP to begin. 6. Once the unit is preheated, spray the crisper plate with cooking oil. Place the chicken into the basket. 7. Select AIR FRY, set the temperature to 190°C, and set the time to 25 minutes. Select START/STOP to begin. 8. After 10 minutes, flip the chicken. Resume cooking. After 10 minutes more, check the chicken. If a food thermometer inserted into the chicken registers 76 ° C and the chicken is brown and crisp, it is done. Otherwise, resume cooking for up to 5 minutes longer. 9. When the cooking is complete, let cool for 5 minutes, then serve.

Lemon-Dijon Boneless Chicken

Prep time: 30 minutes | Cook time: 13 to 16 minutes | Serves 6

115 g sugar-free mayonnaise

1 tablespoon Dijon mustard

1 tablespoon freshly squeezed lemon juice (optional)

1 tablespoon coconut aminos

1 teaspoon Italian seasoning

1 teaspoon sea salt

½ teaspoon freshly ground black pepper

¼ teaspoon cayenne pepper

680 g boneless, skinless chicken breasts or thighs

1. In a small bowl, combine the mayonnaise, mustard, lemon juice (if using), coconut aminos, Italian seasoning, salt, black pepper, and cayenne pepper. 2. Place the chicken in a shallow dish or large zip-top plastic bag. Add the marinade, making sure all the pieces are coated. Cover and refrigerate for at least 30 minutes or up to 4 hours. 3. Set the air fryer to 200°C. Arrange the chicken in a single layer in the air fryer basket, working in batches if necessary. Air fry for 7 minutes. Flip the chicken and continue cooking for 6 to 9 minutes more, until an instant-read thermometer reads 70°C.

Spice-Rubbed Chicken Thighs

Prep time: 10 minutes | Cook time: 25 minutes | Serves 4

4 (115 g) bone-in, skin-on chicken thighs

½ teaspoon salt

½ teaspoon garlic powder

2 teaspoons chilli powder

1 teaspoon paprika

1 teaspoon ground cumin

1 small lime, halved

1. Pat chicken thighs dry and sprinkle with salt, garlic powder, chilli powder, paprika, and cumin. 2. Squeeze juice from ½ lime over thighs. Place thighs into ungreased air fryer basket. Adjust the temperature to 190°C and roast for 25 minutes, turning thighs halfway through cooking. Thighs will be crispy and browned with an internal temperature of at least 76 ° C when done. 3. Transfer thighs to a large serving plate and

drizzle with remaining lime juice. Serve warm.

Italian Chicken with Sauce

Prep time: 15 minutes | Cook time: 20 minutes | Serves 4

2 large skinless chicken breasts (about 565 g)

Salt and freshly ground black pepper

25 g ground almonds

45 g grated Parmesan cheese

2 teaspoons Italian seasoning

1 egg, lightly beaten

1 tablespoon olive oil

225 g no-sugar-added marinara sauce

4 slices Mozzarella cheese or 110 g shredded Mozzarella

1. Preheat the air fryer to 180°C. 2. Slice the chicken breasts in half horizontally to create 4 thinner chicken breasts. Working with one piece at a time, place the chicken between two pieces of parchment paper and pound with a meat mallet or rolling pin to flatten to an even thickness. Season both sides with salt and freshly ground black pepper. 3. In a large shallow bowl, combine the ground almonds, Parmesan, and Italian seasoning; stir until thoroughly combined. Place the egg in another large shallow bowl. 4. Dip the chicken in the egg, followed by the ground almonds mixture, pressing the mixture firmly into the chicken to create an even coating. 5. Working in batches if necessary, arrange the chicken breasts in a single layer in the air fryer basket and coat both sides lightly with olive oil. Pausing halfway through the cooking time to flip the chicken, air fry for 15 minutes, or until a thermometer inserted into the thickest part registers 76°C. 6. Spoon the marinara sauce over each piece of chicken and top with the Mozzarella cheese. Air fry for an additional 3 to 5 minutes until the cheese is melted.

Thai-Style Cornish Game Hens

Prep time: 30 minutes | Cook time: 20 minutes | Serves 4

20 g chopped fresh coriander leaves and stems

60 ml fish sauce

1 tablespoon soy sauce

1 serrano chilli, seeded and chopped

8 garlic cloves, smashed

2 tablespoons sugar

2 tablespoons lemongrass paste

2 teaspoons black pepper

2 teaspoons ground coriander

1 teaspoon kosher salt

1 teaspoon ground turmeric

2 Cornish game hens, giblets removed, split in half lengthwise

1. In a blender, combine the coriander, fish sauce, soy sauce, serrano, garlic, sugar, lemongrass, black pepper, coriander, salt, and turmeric. Blend until smooth. 2. Place the game hen halves in a large bowl. Pour the coriander mixture over the hen halves and toss to coat. Marinate at room temperature for 30 minutes, or cover and refrigerate for up to 24 hours. 3. Arrange the hen halves in a single layer in the air fryer basket. Set the air fryer to 200 ° C for 20 minutes. Use a meat thermometer to ensure the game hens have reached an internal temperature of 76°C.

Cajun-Breaded Chicken Bites

Prep time: 10 minutes | Cook time: 12 minutes | Serves 4

450 g boneless, skinless chicken breasts, cut into 1-inch cubes

120 g heavy whipping cream

½ teaspoon salt

¼ teaspoon ground black pepper

30 g plain pork rinds, finely crushed

40 g unflavoured whey protein powder

½ teaspoon Cajun seasoning

1. Place chicken in a medium bowl and pour in cream. Stir to coat. Sprinkle with salt and pepper. 2. In a separate large bowl, combine pork rinds, protein powder, and Cajun seasoning. Remove chicken from cream, shaking off any excess, and toss in dry mix until fully coated. 3. Place bites into ungreased air fryer basket. Adjust the temperature to 200°C and air fry for 12 minutes, shaking the basket twice during cooking. Bites will be done when golden brown and have an internal temperature of at least 76°C. Serve warm.

Gold Livers

Prep time: 10 minutes | Cook time: 20 minutes | Serves 4

2 eggs

2 tablespoons water

45 g flour

120 g panko breadcrumbs

1 teaspoon salt

½ teaspoon ground black pepper

570 g chicken livers

Cooking spray

1. Preheat the air fryer to 200°C. Spritz the air fryer basket with cooking spray. 2. Whisk the eggs with water in a large bowl. Pour the flour in a separate bowl. Pour the panko on a shallow dish and sprinkle with salt and pepper. 3. Dredge the chicken livers in the flour. Shake the excess off, then dunk the livers in the whisked eggs, and then roll the livers over the panko to coat well. 4. Arrange the livers in the preheated air

fryer and spritz with cooking spray. Work in batches to avoid overcrowding. 5. Air fry for 10 minutes or until the livers are golden and crispy. Flip the livers halfway through. Repeat with remaining livers. 6. Serve immediately.

Buffalo Chicken Cheese Sticks

Prep time: 5 minutes | Cook time: 8 minutes | Serves 2

140 g shredded cooked chicken

60 ml buffalo sauce

220 g shredded Mozzarella cheese

1 large egg

55 g crumbled feta

1. In a large bowl, mix all ingredients except the feta. Cut a piece of parchment to fit your air fryer basket and press the mixture into a ½-inch-thick circle. 2. Sprinkle the mixture with feta and place into the air fryer basket. 3. Adjust the temperature to 200ºC and air fry for 8 minutes. 4. After 5 minutes, flip over the cheese mixture. 5. Allow to cool 5 minutes before cutting into sticks. Serve warm.

Coriander Lime Chicken Thighs

Prep time: 15 minutes | Cook time: 22 minutes | Serves 4

4 bone-in, skin-on chicken thighs

1 teaspoon baking powder

½ teaspoon garlic powder

2 teaspoons chilli powder

1 teaspoon cumin

2 medium limes

5 g chopped fresh coriander

1. Pat chicken thighs dry and sprinkle with baking powder. 2. In a small bowl, mix garlic powder, chilli powder, and cumin and sprinkle evenly over thighs,

gently rubbing on and under chicken skin. 3. Cut one lime in half and squeeze juice over thighs. Place chicken into the air fryer basket. 4. Adjust the temperature to 190°C and roast for 22 minutes. 5. Cut other lime into four wedges for serving and garnish cooked chicken with wedges and coriander.

Juicy Paprika Chicken Breast

Prep time: 5 minutes | Cook time: 30 minutes | Serves 4

Oil, for spraying

4 (170 g) boneless, skinless chicken breasts

1 tablespoon olive oil

1 tablespoon paprika

1 tablespoon packed light brown sugar

½ teaspoon cayenne pepper

½ teaspoon onion powder

½ teaspoon granulated garlic

1. Line the air fryer basket with parchment and spray lightly with oil. 2. Brush the chicken with the olive oil. 3. In a small bowl, mix together the paprika, brown sugar, cayenne pepper, onion powder, and garlic and sprinkle it over the chicken. 4. Place the chicken in the prepared basket. You may need to work in batches, depending on the size of your air fryer. 5. Air fry at 180 °C for 15 minutes, flip, and cook for another 15 minutes, or until the internal temperature reaches 76°C. Serve immediately.

Chapter 5 Beef, Pork, and Lamb

Spicy Rump Steak

Prep time: 25 minutes | Cook time: 12 to 18 minutes | Serves 4

2 tablespoons salsa

1 tablespoon minced chipotle pepper or chipotle paste

1 tablespoon apple cider vinegar

1 teaspoon ground cumin

⅛ teaspoon freshly ground black pepper

⅛ teaspoon red pepper flakes

340 g rump steak, cut into 4 pieces and gently pounded to about ⅓ inch thick

Cooking oil spray

1. In a small bowl, thoroughly mix the salsa, chipotle pepper, vinegar, cumin, black pepper, and red pepper flakes. Rub this mixture into both sides of each steak piece. Let stand for 15 minutes at room temperature. 2. Insert the crisper plate into the basket and place the basket into the unit. Preheat the unit by selecting AIR FRY, setting the temperature to 200°C, and setting the time to 3 minutes. Select START/STOP to begin. 3. Once the unit is preheated, spray the crisper plate with cooking oil. Working in batches, place 2 steaks into the basket. 4. Select AIR FRY, set the temperature to 200°C, and set the time to 9 minutes. Select START/STOP to begin. 5. After about 6 minutes, check the steaks. If a food thermometer inserted into the meat registers at least 64°C, they are done. If not, resume cooking. 6. When the cooking is done, transfer the steaks to a clean plate and cover with aluminium foil to keep warm. Repeat steps 3, 4, and 5 with the remaining steaks. 7. Thinly slice the steaks against the grain and serve.

Jalapeño Popper Pork Chops

Prep time: 15 minutes | Cook time: 6 to 8 minutes | Serves 4

800 g bone-in, loin pork chops

Sea salt and freshly ground black pepper, to taste

170 g cream cheese, at room temperature

110 g sliced bacon, cooked and crumbled

110 g Cheddar cheese, shredded

1 jalapeño, seeded and diced

1 teaspoon garlic powder

1. Cut a pocket into each pork chop, lengthwise along the side, making sure not to cut it all the way through. Season the outside of the chops with salt and pepper. 2. In a small bowl, combine the cream cheese, bacon, Cheddar cheese, jalapeño, and garlic powder. Divide this mixture among the pork chops, stuffing it into the pocket of each chop. 3. Set the air fryer to 200°C. Place the pork chops in the air fryer basket in a single layer, working in batches if necessary. Air fry for 3 minutes. Flip the chops and cook for 3 to 5 minutes more, until an instant-read thermometer reads 64°C. 4. Allow the chops to rest for 5 minutes, then serve warm.

Minute Steak Roll-Ups

Prep time: 30 minutes | Cook time: 8 to 10 minutes | Serves 4

4 minute steaks (170 g each)

1 (450 g) bottle Italian dressing

1 teaspoon salt

½ teaspoon freshly ground black pepper

120 g finely chopped brown onion

120 g finely chopped green pepper

120 g finely chopped mushrooms

1 to 2 tablespoons oil

1. In a large resealable bag or airtight storage container, combine the steaks and Italian dressing. Seal the bag and refrigerate to marinate for 2 hours. 2. Remove the steaks from the marinade and place them on a cutting board. Discard the marinade. Evenly season the steaks with salt and pepper. 3. In a small bowl, stir together the onion, pepper, and mushrooms. Sprinkle the onion mixture evenly over the steaks. Roll up the steaks, jam roll-style, and secure with toothpicks. 4. Preheat the air fryer to 200 °C. 5. Place the steaks in the air fryer basket. 6. Cook for 4 minutes. Flip the steaks and spritz them with oil. Cook for 4 to 6 minutes more until the internal temperature reaches 64 °C. Let rest for 5 minutes before serving.

Tomato and Bacon Zoodles

Prep time: 10 minutes | Cook time: 15 to 22 minutes | Serves 2

230 g sliced bacon

120 g baby plum tomatoes

1 large courgette, spiralized

120 g ricotta cheese

60 ml double/whipping cream

80 g finely grated Parmesan cheese, plus more for serving

Sea salt and freshly ground black pepper, to taste

1. Set the air fryer to 200°C. Arrange the bacon strips in a single layer in the air fryer basket — some overlapping is okay because the bacon will shrink, but cook in batches if needed. Air fry for 8 minutes. Flip the bacon strips and air fry for 2 to 5 minutes more, until the bacon is crisp. Remove the bacon from the air fryer. 2. Put the tomatoes in the air fryer basket and air fry for 3 to 5 minutes, until they are just starting to burst. Remove the tomatoes from the air fryer. 3. Put

the courgette noodles in the air fryer and air fry for 2 to 4 minutes, to the desired doneness. 4. Meanwhile, combine the ricotta, cream, and Parmesan in a saucepan over medium-low heat. Cook, stirring often, until warm and combined. 5. Crumble the bacon. Place the courgette, bacon, and tomatoes in a bowl. Toss with the ricotta sauce. Season with salt and pepper, and sprinkle with additional Parmesan.

Roast Beef with Horseradish Cream

Prep time: 5 minutes | Cook time: 35 to 45 minutes | Serves 6

900 g beef roasting joint

1 tablespoon salt

2 teaspoons garlic powder

1 teaspoon freshly ground black pepper

1 teaspoon dried thyme

Horseradish Cream:

80 ml double cream

80 ml sour cream

80 g grated horseradish

2 teaspoons fresh lemon juice

Salt and freshly ground black pepper, to taste

1. Preheat the air fryer to 200 °C. 2. Season the beef with the salt, garlic powder, black pepper, and thyme. Place the beef fat-side down in the basket of the air fryer and lightly coat with olive oil. Pausing halfway through the cooking time to turn the meat, air fry for 35 to 45 minutes, until a thermometer inserted into the thickest part indicates the desired doneness, 52ºC (rare) to 64 °C (medium). Let the beef rest for 10 minutes before slicing. 3. To make the horseradish cream: In a small bowl, combine the double cream, sour cream, horseradish, and lemon juice. Whisk until thoroughly combined. Season to taste with salt and freshly ground

black pepper. Serve alongside the beef.

Almond and Caraway Crust Steak

Prep time: 16 minutes | Cook time: 10 minutes | Serves 4

40 g almond flour

2 eggs

2 teaspoons caraway seeds

4 beef steaks

2 teaspoons garlic powder

1 tablespoon melted butter

Fine sea salt and cayenne pepper, to taste

1. Generously coat steaks with garlic powder, caraway seeds, salt, and cayenne pepper. 2. In a mixing dish, thoroughly combine melted butter with seasoned crumbs. In another bowl, beat the eggs until they're well whisked. 3. First, coat steaks with the beaten egg; then, coat beef steaks with the buttered crumb mixture. Place the steaks in the air fryer basket; cook for 10 minutes at 180ºC. Bon appétit!

Honey-Baked Pork Loin

Prep time: 30 minutes | Cook time: 22 to 25 minutes | Serves 6

60 ml honey

60 g freshly squeezed lemon juice

2 tablespoons soy sauce

1 teaspoon garlic powder

1 (900 g) pork loin

2 tablespoons vegetable oil

1. In a medium bowl, whisk together the honey, lemon juice, soy sauce, and garlic powder. Reserve half of the mixture for basting during cooking. 2. Cut 5 slits in the pork loin and transfer it to a resealable bag. Add the remaining honey mixture. Seal the bag and refrigerate

to marinate for at least 2 hours. 3. Preheat the air fryer to 200 º C. Line the air fryer basket with parchment paper. 4. Remove the pork from the marinade, and place it on the parchment. Spritz with oil, then baste with the reserved marinade. 5. Cook for 15 minutes. Flip the pork, baste with more marinade and spritz with oil again. Cook for 7 to 10 minutes more until the internal temperature reaches 64 º C. Let rest for 5 minutes before serving.

Chinese-Style Pork Loin Back Ribs

Prep time: 30 minutes | Cook time: 30 minutes | Serves 4

1 tablespoon toasted sesame oil

1 tablespoon fermented black bean paste

1 tablespoon Shaoxing wine (rice cooking wine)

1 tablespoon dark soy sauce

1 tablespoon agave nectar or honey

1 teaspoon minced garlic

1 teaspoon minced fresh ginger

1 (680 g) slab pork loin Back Ribs, cut into individual ribs

1. In a large bowl, stir together the sesame oil, black bean paste, wine, soy sauce, agave, garlic, and ginger. Add the ribs and toss well to coat. Marinate at room temperature for 30 minutes, or cover and refrigerate for up to 24 hours. 2. Place the ribs in the air fryer basket; discard the marinade. Set the air fryer to 180ºC for 30 minutes.

Garlic Balsamic London Broil

Prep time: 30 minutes | Cook time: 8 to 10 minutes | Serves 8

900 g bavette or skirt steak

3 large garlic cloves, minced

3 tablespoons balsamic vinegar

3 tablespoons wholegrain mustard

2 tablespoons olive oil

Sea salt and ground black pepper, to taste

½ teaspoon dried hot red pepper flakes

1. Score both sides of the cleaned steak. 2. Thoroughly combine the remaining ingredients; massage this mixture into the meat to coat it on all sides. Let it marinate for at least 3 hours. 3. Set the air fryer to 200° C; Then cook the steak for 15 minutes. Flip it over and cook another 10 to 12 minutes. Bon appétit!

Italian Pork Loin

Prep time: 30 minutes | Cook time: 16 minutes | Serves 3

1 teaspoon sea salt

½ teaspoon black pepper, freshly cracked

60 ml red wine

2 tablespoons mustard

2 garlic cloves, minced

450 g pork loin joint

1 tablespoon Italian herb seasoning blend

1. In a ceramic bowl, mix the salt, black pepper, red wine, mustard, and garlic. Add the pork loin and let it marinate at least 30 minutes. 2. Spritz the sides and bottom of the air fryer basket with nonstick cooking spray. 3. Place the pork loin in the basket; sprinkle with the Italian herb seasoning blend. Cook the pork loin at 190°C for 10 minutes. Flip halfway through, spraying with cooking oil and cook for 5 to 6 minutes more. Serve immediately.

Pork Tenderloin with Avocado Lime Sauce

Prep time: 30 minutes | Cook time: 15 minutes | Serves 4

Marinade:

120 ml lime juice

Grated zest of 1 lime

2 teaspoons stevia glycerite, or ¼ teaspoon liquid stevia

3 cloves garlic, minced

1½ teaspoons fine sea salt

1 teaspoon chilli powder, or more for more heat

1 teaspoon smoked paprika

450 g pork tenderloin

Avocado Lime Sauce:

1 medium-sized ripe avocado, roughly chopped

120 ml full-fat sour cream (or coconut cream for dairy-free)

Grated zest of 1 lime

Juice of 1 lime

2 cloves garlic, roughly chopped

½ teaspoon fine sea salt

¼ teaspoon ground black pepper

Chopped fresh coriander leaves, for garnish

Lime slices, for serving

Pico de gallo or salsa, for serving

1. In a medium-sized casserole dish, stir together all the marinade ingredients until well combined. Add the tenderloin and coat it well in the marinade. Cover and place in the fridge to marinate for 2 hours or overnight. 2. Spray the air fryer basket with avocado oil. Preheat the air fryer to 200°C. 3. Remove the pork from the marinade and place it in the air fryer basket. Air fry for 13 to 15 minutes, until the internal temperature of the pork is 64°C, flipping after 7 minutes. Remove the pork from the air fryer and place it on a cutting board. Allow it to rest for 8 to 10 minutes, then cut it into ½

-inch-thick slices. 4. While the pork cooks, make the avocado lime sauce: Place all the sauce ingredients in a food processor and purée until smooth. Taste and adjust the seasoning to your liking. 5. Place the pork slices on a serving platter and spoon the avocado lime sauce on top. Garnish with coriander leaves and serve with lime slices and pico de gallo. 6. Store leftovers in an airtight container in the fridge for up to 4 days. Reheat in a preheated 200ºC air fryer for 5 minutes, or until heated through.

Rosemary Ribeye Steaks

Prep time: 10 minutes | Cook time: 15 minutes | Serves 2

60 g butter

1 clove garlic, minced

Salt and ground black pepper, to taste

1½ tablespoons balsamic vinegar

60 g rosemary, chopped

2 ribeye steaks

1. Melt the butter in a frying pan over medium heat. Add the garlic and fry until fragrant. 2. Remove the frying pan from the heat and add the salt, pepper, and vinegar. Allow it to cool. 3. Add the rosemary, then pour the mixture into a Ziploc bag. 4. Put the ribeye steaks in the bag and shake well, coating the meat well. Refrigerate for an hour, then allow to sit for a further twenty minutes. 5. Preheat the air fryer to 200ºC. 6. Air fry the ribeye steaks for 15 minutes. 7. Take care when removing the steaks from the air fryer and plate up. 8. Serve immediately.

Air Fried Beef Satay with Peanut Dipping Sauce

Prep time: 30 minutes | Cook time: 5 to 7 minutes | Serves 4

230 g bavette or skirt steak, sliced into 8 strips

2 teaspoons curry powder

½ teaspoon coarse or flaky salt

Cooking spray

Peanut Dipping sauce:

2 tablespoons creamy peanut butter

1 tablespoon reduced-salt soy sauce

2 teaspoons rice vinegar

1 teaspoon honey

1 teaspoon grated ginger

Special Equipment:

4 bamboo skewers, cut into halves and soaked in water for 20 minutes to keep them from burning while cooking

1. Preheat the air fryer to 180°C. Spritz the air fryer basket with cooking spray. 2. In a bowl, place the steak strips and sprinkle with the curry powder and coarse or flaky salt to season. Thread the strips onto the soaked skewers. 3. Arrange the skewers in the prepared air fryer basket and spritz with cooking spray. Air fry for 5 to 7 minutes, or until the beef is well browned, turning halfway through. 4. In the meantime, stir together the peanut butter, soy sauce, rice vinegar, honey, and ginger in a bowl to make the dipping sauce. 5. Transfer the beef to the serving dishes and let rest for 5 minutes. Serve with the peanut dipping sauce on the side.

Hoisin BBQ Pork Chops

Prep time: 5 minutes | Cook time: 22 minutes | Serves 2 to 3

3 tablespoons hoisin sauce

60 ml honey

1 tablespoon soy sauce

3 tablespoons rice vinegar

2 tablespoons brown sugar

1½ teaspoons grated fresh ginger

1 to 2 teaspoons Sriracha sauce, to taste

2 to 3 bone-in pork chops, 1-inch thick (about 567 g)

Chopped spring onionspring onions, for garnish

1. Combine the hoisin sauce, honey, soy sauce, rice vinegar, brown sugar, ginger, and Sriracha sauce in a small saucepan. Whisk the ingredients together and bring the mixture to a boil over medium-high heat on the stovetop. Reduce the heat and simmer the sauce until it has reduced in volume and thickened slightly, about 10 minutes. 2. Preheat the air fryer to 200°C. 3. Place the pork chops into the air fryer basket and pour half the hoisin BBQ sauce over the top. Air fry for 6 minutes. Then, flip the chops over, pour the remaining hoisin BBQ sauce on top and air fry for 5 to 6 more minutes, depending on the thickness of the pork chops. The internal temperature of the pork chops should be 68°C when tested with an instant read thermometer. 4. Let the pork chops rest for 5 minutes before serving. You can spoon a little of the sauce from the bottom drawer of the air fryer over the top if desired. Sprinkle with chopped spring onionspring onions and serve.

Pork and Tricolor Vegetables Kebabs

Prep time: 1 hour 20 minutes | Cook time: 8 minutes per batch | Serves 4

For the Pork:

450 g pork steak, cut in cubes

1 tablespoon white wine vinegar

3 tablespoons steak sauce or brown sauce

60 ml soy sauce

1 teaspoon powdered chili

1 teaspoon red chilli flakes

2 teaspoons smoked paprika

1 teaspoon garlic salt

For the Vegetable:

1 courgette, cut in cubes

1 butternut marrow, deseeded and cut in cubes

1 red pepper, cut in cubes

1 green pepper, cut in cubes

Salt and ground black pepper, to taste

Cooking spray

Special Equipment:

4 bamboo skewers, soaked in water for at least 30 minutes

1. Combine the ingredients for the pork in a large bowl. Press the pork to dunk in the marinade. Wrap the bowl in plastic and refrigerate for at least an hour. 2. Preheat the air fryer to 190°C and spritz with cooking spray. 3. Remove the pork from the marinade and run the skewers through the pork and vegetables alternatively. Sprinkle with salt and pepper to taste. 4. Arrange the skewers in the preheated air fryer and spritz with cooking spray. Air fry for 8 minutes or until the pork is browned and the vegetables are lightly charred and tender. Flip the skewers halfway through. You may need to work in batches to avoid overcrowding. 5. Serve immediately.

Kheema Burgers

Prep time: 15 minutes | Cook time: 12 minutes | Serves 4

Burgers:

450 g 85% lean beef mince or lamb mince

2 large eggs, lightly beaten

1 medium brown onion, diced

60 g chopped fresh coriander

1 tablespoon minced fresh ginger

3 cloves garlic, minced

2 teaspoons garam masala

1 teaspoon ground turmeric

½ teaspoon ground cinnamon

⅛ teaspoon ground cardamom

1 teaspoon coarse or flaky salt

1 teaspoon cayenne pepper

Raita Sauce:

235 g grated cucumber

120 ml sour cream

¼ teaspoon coarse or flaky salt

¼ teaspoon black pepper

For Serving:

4 lettuce leaves, hamburger buns, or naan breads

1. For the burgers: In a large bowl, combine the beef mince, eggs, onion, coriander, ginger, garlic, garam masala, turmeric, cinnamon, cardamom, salt, and cayenne. Gently mix until ingredients are thoroughly combined. 2. Divide the meat into four portions and form into round patties. Make a slight depression in the middle of each patty with your thumb to prevent them from puffing up into a dome shape while cooking. 3. Place the patties in the air fryer basket. Set the air fryer to 180°C for 12 minutes. Use a meat thermometer to ensure the burgers have reached an internal temperature of 72°C (for medium). 4. Meanwhile, for the sauce: In a small bowl, combine the cucumber, sour cream, salt, and pepper. 5. To serve: Place the burgers on the lettuce, buns, or naan and top with the sauce.

Panko Pork Chops

Prep time: 10 minutes | Cook time: 12 minutes | Serves 4

4 boneless pork chops, excess fat trimmed

¼ teaspoon salt

2 eggs

130 g panko bread crumbs

3 tablespoons grated Parmesan cheese

1½ teaspoons paprika

½ teaspoon granulated garlic

½ teaspoon onion granules

1 teaspoon chilli powder

¼ teaspoon freshly ground black pepper

Olive oil spray

1. Sprinkle the pork chops with salt on both sides and let them sit while you prepare the seasonings and egg wash. 2. In a shallow medium bowl, beat the eggs. 3. In another shallow medium bowl, stir together the panko, Parmesan cheese, paprika, granulated garlic, onion granules, chilli powder, and pepper. 4. Dip the pork chops in the egg and in the panko mixture to coat. Firmly press the crumbs onto the chops. 5. Insert the crisper plate into the basket and the basket into the unit. Preheat the unit by selecting AIR ROAST, setting the temperature to 200°C, and setting the time to 3 minutes. Select START/STOP to begin. 6. Once the unit is preheated, spray the crisper plate with olive oil. Place the pork chops into the basket and spray them with olive oil. 7. Select AIR ROAST, set the temperature to 200 ° C, and set the time to 12 minutes. Select START/STOP to begin. 8. After 6 minutes, flip the pork chops and spray them with more olive oil. Resume cooking. 9. When the cooking is complete, the chops should be golden and crispy and a food thermometer should register 64°C. Serve immediately.

Easy Beef Satay

Prep time: 30 minutes | Cook time: 8 minutes | Serves 4

450 g beef bavette or skirt steak, thinly sliced into long strips

2 tablespoons vegetable oil

1 tablespoon fish sauce

1 tablespoon soy sauce

1 tablespoon minced fresh ginger

1 tablespoon minced garlic

1 tablespoon sugar

1 teaspoon Sriracha or other hot sauce

1 teaspoon ground coriander

120 g chopped fresh coriander

60 g chopped roasted peanuts

1. Place the beef strips in a large bowl or resealable plastic bag. Add the vegetable oil, fish sauce, soy sauce, ginger, garlic, sugar, Sriracha, coriander, and 60 ml of the fresh coriander to the bag. Seal and massage the bag to thoroughly coat and combine. Marinate at room temperature for 30 minutes, or cover and refrigerate for up to 24 hours. 2. Using tongs, remove the beef strips from the bag and lay them flat in the air fryer basket, minimizing overlap as much as possible; discard the marinade. Set the air fryer to 200 °C for 8 minutes, turning the beef strips halfway through the cooking time. 3. Transfer the meat to a serving platter. Sprinkle with the remaining 60 ml coriander and the peanuts. Serve.

Kale and Beef Omelet

Prep time: 15 minutes | Cook time: 16 minutes | Serves 4

230 g leftover beef, coarsely chopped

2 garlic cloves, pressed

235 g kale, torn into pieces and wilted

1 tomato, chopped

¼ teaspoon sugar

4 eggs, beaten

4 tablespoons double cream

½ teaspoon turmeric powder

Salt and ground black pepper, to taste

⅛ teaspoon ground allspice

Cooking spray

1. Preheat the air fryer to 180°C. Spritz four ramekins with cooking spray. 2. Put equal amounts of each of the ingredients into each ramekin and mix well. 3. Air fry for 16 minutes. Serve immediately.

Rosemary Roast Beef

Prep time: 30 minutes | Cook time: 30 to 35 minutes | Serves 8

1 (900 g) beef roasting joint, tied with kitchen string

Sea salt and freshly ground black pepper, to taste

2 teaspoons minced garlic

2 tablespoons finely chopped fresh rosemary

60 ml avocado oil

1. Season the roast generously with salt and pepper. 2. In a small bowl, whisk together the garlic, rosemary, and avocado oil. Rub this all over the roast. Cover loosely with aluminium foil or cling film and refrigerate for at least 12 hours or up to 2 days. 3. Remove the roast from the refrigerator and allow to sit at room temperature for about 1 hour. 4. Set the air fryer to 160°C. Place the roast in the air fryer basket and roast for 15 minutes. Flip the roast and cook for 15 to 20 minutes more, until the meat is browned and an instant-read thermometer reads 49 °C at the thickest part (for medium-rare). 5. Transfer the meat to a cutting board, and let it rest for 15 minutes before thinly slicing and serving.

Fajita Meatball Lettuce Wraps

Prep time: 10 minutes | Cook time: 10 minutes | Serves 4

450 g beef mince (85% lean)

120 ml salsa, plus more for serving if desired

60 g chopped onions

60 g diced green or red peppers

1 large egg, beaten

1 teaspoon fine sea salt

½ teaspoon chilli powder

½ teaspoon ground cumin

1 clove garlic, minced

For Serving (Optional):

8 leaves butterhead lettuce

Pico de gallo or salsa

Lime slices

1. Spray the air fryer basket with avocado oil. Preheat the air fryer to 180ºC. 2. In a large bowl, mix together all the ingredients until well combined. 3. Shape the meat mixture into eight 1-inch balls. Place the meatballs in the air fryer basket, leaving a little space between them. Air fry for 10 minutes, or until cooked through and no longer pink inside and the internal temperature reaches 64ºC. 4. Serve each meatball on a lettuce leaf, topped with pico de gallo or salsa, if desired. Serve with lime slices if desired. 5. Store leftovers in an airtight container in the fridge for 3 days or in the freezer for up to a month. Reheat in a preheated 180ºC air fryer for 4 minutes, or until heated through.

Bone-in Pork Chops

Prep time: 5 minutes | Cook time: 10 to 12 minutes | Serves 2

450 g bone-in pork chops

1 tablespoon avocado oil

1 teaspoon smoked paprika

½ teaspoon onion granules

¼ teaspoon cayenne pepper

Sea salt and freshly ground black pepper, to taste

1. Brush the pork chops with the avocado oil. In a small dish, mix together the smoked paprika, onion granules, cayenne pepper, and salt and black pepper to taste. Sprinkle the seasonings over both sides of the pork chops. 2. Set the air fryer to 200 ° C. Place the chops in the air fryer basket in a single layer, working in batches if necessary. Air fry for 10 to 12 minutes, until an instant-read thermometer reads 64 ° C at the chops' thickest point. 3. Remove the chops from the air fryer and allow them to rest for 5 minutes before serving.

Banger and Peppers

Prep time: 7 minutes | Cook time: 35 minutes | Serves 4

Oil, for spraying

900 g hot or sweet Italian-seasoned banger links, cut into thick slices

4 large peppers of any color, seeded and cut into slices

1 onion, thinly sliced

1 tablespoon olive oil

1 tablespoon chopped fresh parsley

1 teaspoon dried oregano

1 teaspoon dried basil

1 teaspoon balsamic vinegar

1. Line the air fryer basket with parchment and spray lightly with oil. 2. In a large bowl, combine the banger, peppers, and onion. 3. In a small bowl, whisk together the olive oil, parsley, oregano, basil, and balsamic vinegar. Pour the mixture over the banger and peppers and toss until evenly coated. 4. Using a slotted spoon, transfer the mixture to the prepared basket, taking care to drain out as much excess liquid as possible. 5. Air fry at 180ºC for 20 minutes, stir, and cook for another 15 minutes, or until the banger is browned and the juices run clear.

Pork Medallions with Endive Salad

Prep time: 25 minutes | Cook time: 7 minutes | Serves 4

1 (230 g) pork tenderloin

Salt and freshly ground black pepper, to taste

30 g flour

2 eggs, lightly beaten

180 g finely crushed crackers

1 teaspoon paprika

1 teaspoon mustard powder

1 teaspoon garlic powder

1 teaspoon dried thyme

1 teaspoon salt

vegetable or rapeseed oil, in spray bottle

Vinaigrette:

60 ml white balsamic vinegar

2 tablespoons agave syrup (or honey or maple syrup)

1 tablespoon Dijon mustard

juice of ½ lemon

2 tablespoons chopped chervil or flat-leaf parsley

salt and freshly ground black pepper

120 ml extra-virgin olive oil

Endive Salad:

1 heart romaine lettuce, torn into large pieces

2 heads endive, sliced

120 g cherry tomatoes, halved

85 g fresh Mozzarella, diced

Salt and freshly ground black pepper, to taste

1. Slice the pork tenderloin into 1-inch slices. Using a meat pounder, pound the pork slices into thin ½-inch medallions. Generously season the pork with salt and freshly ground black pepper on both sides. 2. Set up a dredging station using three shallow dishes. Put the flour in one dish and the beaten eggs in a second dish. Combine the crushed crackers, paprika, mustard powder, garlic powder, thyme and salt in a third dish. 3. Preheat the air fryer to 200 °C. 4. Dredge the pork medallions in flour first and then into the beaten egg. Let the excess egg drip off and coat both sides of the medallions with the cracker crumb mixture. Spray both sides of the coated medallions with vegetable or rapeseed oil. 5. Air fry the medallions in two batches at 200°C for 5 minutes. Once you have air-fried all the medallions, flip them all over and return the first batch of medallions back into the air fryer on top of the second batch. Air fry at 200 °C for an additional 2 minutes. 6. While the medallions are cooking, make the salad and dressing. Whisk the white balsamic vinegar, agave syrup, Dijon mustard, lemon juice, chervil, salt and pepper together in a small bowl. Whisk in the olive oil slowly until combined and thickened. 7. Combine the romaine lettuce, endive, cherry tomatoes, and Mozzarella cheese in a large salad bowl. Drizzle the dressing over the vegetables and toss to combine. Season with salt and freshly ground black pepper. 8. Serve the pork medallions warm on or beside the salad.

Mediterranean Beef Steaks

Prep time: 20 minutes | Cook time: 20 minutes | Serves 4

2 tablespoons soy sauce or tamari

3 heaping tablespoons fresh chives

2 tablespoons olive oil

3 tablespoons dry white wine

4 small-sized beef steaks

2 teaspoons smoked cayenne pepper

½ teaspoon dried basil

½ teaspoon dried rosemary

1 teaspoon freshly ground black pepper

1 teaspoon sea salt, or more to taste

1. Firstly, coat the steaks with the cayenne pepper, black pepper, salt, basil, and rosemary. 2. Drizzle the steaks with olive oil, white wine, and soy sauce. 3. Finally, roast in the air fryer for 20 minutes at 170°C. Serve garnished with fresh chives. Bon appétit!

Indian Mint and Chile Kebabs

Prep time: 30 minutes | Cook time: 15 minutes | Serves 4

450 g lamb mince

120 g finely minced onion

60 g chopped fresh mint

60 g chopped fresh coriander

1 tablespoon minced garlic

½ teaspoon ground turmeric

½ teaspoon cayenne pepper

¼ teaspoon ground cardamom

¼ teaspoon ground cinnamon

1 teaspoon coarse or flaky salt

1. In the bowl of a stand mixer fitted with the paddle attachment, combine the lamb, onion, mint, coriander, garlic, turmeric, cayenne, cardamom, cinnamon, and salt. Mix on low speed until you have a sticky mess of spiced meat. If you have time, let the mixture stand at room temperature for 30 minutes (or cover and refrigerate for up to a day or two, until you're ready to make the kebabs). 2. Divide the meat into eight equal portions. Form each into a long banger shape. Place the kebabs in a single layer in the air fryer basket. Set the air fryer to 180°C for 10 minutes. Increase the air fryer temperature to 200°C and cook for 3 to 4 minutes more

to brown the kebabs. Use a meat thermometer to ensure the kebabs have reached an internal temperature of 72°C (medium).

Beef and Pork Banger Meatloaf

Prep time: 20 minutes | Cook time: 25 minutes | Serves 4

340 g beef mince

110 g pork banger meat

235 g shallots, finely chopped

2 eggs, well beaten

3 tablespoons milk

1 tablespoon oyster sauce

1 teaspoon porcini mushrooms

½ teaspoon cumin powder

1 teaspoon garlic paste

1 tablespoon fresh parsley

Salt and crushed red pepper flakes, to taste

235 g crushed cream crackers

Cooking spray

1. Preheat the air fryer to 180°C. Spritz a baking dish with cooking spray. 2. Mix all the ingredients in a large bowl, combining everything well. 3. Transfer to the baking dish and bake in the air fryer for 25 minutes. 4. Serve hot.

Caraway Crusted Beef Steaks

Prep time: 5 minutes | Cook time: 10 minutes | Serves 4

4 beef steaks

2 teaspoons caraway seeds

2 teaspoons garlic powder

Sea salt and cayenne pepper, to taste

1 tablespoon melted butter

40 g almond flour

2 eggs, beaten

1. Preheat the air fryer to 180ºC. 2. Add the beef steaks to a large bowl and toss with the caraway seeds, garlic powder, salt and pepper until well coated. 3. Stir together the melted butter and almond flour in a bowl. Whisk the eggs in a different bowl. 4. Dredge the seasoned steaks in the eggs, then dip in the almond and butter mixture. 5. Arrange the coated steaks in the air fryer basket. Air fryer for 10 minutes, or until the internal temperature of the beef steaks reaches at least 64 ° C on a meat thermometer. Flip the steaks once halfway through to ensure even cooking. 6. Transfer the steaks to plates. Let cool for 5 minutes and serve hot.

Barbecue Ribs

Prep time: 5 minutes | Cook time: 30 minutes | Serves 4

1 (900 g) rack pork loin Back Ribs

1 teaspoon onion granules

1 teaspoon garlic powder

1 teaspoon light brown sugar

1 teaspoon dried oregano

Salt and freshly ground black pepper, to taste

Cooking oil spray

120 ml barbecue sauce

1. Use a sharp knife to remove the thin membrane from the back of the ribs. Cut the rack in half, or as needed, so the ribs fit in the air fryer basket. The best way to do this is to cut the ribs into 4- or 5-rib sections. 2. In a small bowl, stir together the onion granules, garlic powder, brown sugar, and oregano and season with salt and pepper. Rub the spice seasoning onto the front and back of the ribs. 3. Cover the ribs with cling film or

foil and let sit at room temperature for 30 minutes. 4. Insert the crisper plate into the basket and the basket into the unit. Preheat the unit by selecting AIR ROAST, setting the temperature to 180ºC, and setting the time to 3 minutes. Select START/STOP to begin. 5. Once the unit is preheated, spray the crisper plate with cooking oil. Place the ribs into the basket. It is okay to stack them. 6. Select AIR ROAST, set the temperature to 180 ° C, and set the time to 30 minutes. Select START/STOP to begin. 7. After 15 minutes, flip the ribs. Resume cooking for 15 minutes, or until a food thermometer registers 88 ° C. 8. When the cooking is complete, transfer the ribs to a serving dish. Drizzle the ribs with the barbecue sauce and serve.

Mustard Lamb Chops

Prep time: 5 minutes | Cook time: 14 minutes | Serves 4

Oil, for spraying

1 tablespoon Dijon mustard

2 teaspoons lemon juice

½ teaspoon dried tarragon

¼ teaspoon salt

¼ teaspoon freshly ground black pepper

4 (1¼-inch-thick) loin lamb chops

1. Preheat the air fryer to 200 ° C. Line the air fryer basket with parchment and spray lightly with oil. 2. In a small bowl, mix together the mustard, lemon juice, tarragon, salt, and black pepper. 3. Pat dry the lamb chops with a paper towel. Brush the chops on both sides with the mustard mixture. 4. Place the chops in the prepared basket. You may need to work in batches, depending on the size of your air fryer. 5. Cook for 8 minutes, flip, and cook for another 6 minutes, or until the internal temperature reaches 52ºC for rare, 64ºC for medium-rare, or 68ºC for medium.

Chapter 6 Fish and Seafood

Cajun Salmon

Prep time: 5 minutes | Cook time: 7 minutes | Serves 2

2 salmon fillets, skin removed, 100 g each

2 tablespoons unsalted butter, melted

⅛ teaspoon ground cayenne pepper

½ teaspoon garlic powder

1 teaspoon paprika

¼ teaspoon ground black pepper

1. Brush each fillet with butter. 2. Combine remaining ingredients in a small bowl and then rub onto fish. Place fillets into the air fryer basket. 3. Adjust the temperature to 200°C and air fry for 7 minutes. 4. When fully cooked, internal temperature will be 64ºC. Serve immediately.

Coconut Prawns with Pineapple-Lemon Sauce

Prep time: 10 minutes | Cook time: 18 minutes | Serves 4

60 g light brown sugar

2 teaspoons cornflour

⅛ teaspoon plus ½ teaspoon salt, divided

110 g crushed pineapple with syrup

2 tablespoons freshly squeezed lemon juice

1 tablespoon yellow mustard

680 g raw large prawns, peeled and deveined

2 eggs

30 g plain flour

95 g desiccated, unsweetened coconut

¼ teaspoon garlic granules

Olive oil spray

1. In a medium saucepan over medium heat, combine the brown sugar, cornflour, and ⅛ teaspoon of salt. 2. As the brown sugar mixture melts into a sauce, stir in the crushed pineapple with syrup, lemon juice, and mustard. Cook for about 4 minutes until the mixture thickens and begins to boil. Boil for 1 minute. Remove the pan from the heat, set aside, and let cool while you make the prawns. 3. Put the prawns on a plate and pat them dry with paper towels. 4. In a small bowl, whisk the eggs. 5. In a medium bowl, stir together the flour, desiccated coconut, remaining ½ teaspoon of salt, and garlic granules. 6. Insert the crisper plate into the basket and the basket into the unit. Preheat the unit to 200°C. 7. Dip the prawns into the egg and into the coconut mixture to coat. 8. Once the unit is preheated, place a baking paper liner into the basket. Place the coated prawns on the liner in a single layer and spray them with olive oil. 9. After 6 minutes, remove the basket, flip the prawns, and spray them with more olive oil. Reinsert the basket to resume cooking. Check the prawns after 3 minutes more. If browned, they are done; if not, resume cooking. 10. When the cooking is complete, serve with the prepared pineapple sauce.

Lemon-Pepper Trout

Prep time: 5 minutes | Cook time: 15 minutes | Serves 4

4 trout fillets

2 tablespoons olive oil

½ teaspoon salt

1 teaspoon black pepper

2 garlic cloves, sliced

1 lemon, sliced, plus additional wedges for serving

1. Preheat the air fryer to 190°C. 2. Brush each fillet with olive oil on both sides and season with salt and

pepper. Place the fillets in an even layer in the air fryer basket. 3. Place the sliced garlic over the tops of the trout fillets, then top the garlic with lemon slices and roast for 12 to 15 minutes, or until it has reached an internal temperature of 64ºC. 4. Serve with fresh lemon wedges.

Asian Swordfish

Prep time: 10 minutes | Cook time: 6 to 11 minutes | Serves 4

4 swordfish steaks, 100 g each

½ teaspoon toasted sesame oil

1 red chilli, finely minced

2 garlic cloves, grated

1 tablespoon grated fresh ginger

½ teaspoon Chinese five-spice powder

⅛ teaspoon freshly ground black pepper

2 tablespoons freshly squeezed lemon juice

1. Place the swordfish steaks on a work surface and drizzle with the sesame oil. 2. In a small bowl, mix the jalapeño, garlic, ginger, five-spice powder, pepper, and lemon juice. Rub this mixture into the fish and let it stand for 10 minutes. 3. Roast the swordfish in the air fryer at 190 º C for 6 to 11 minutes, or until the swordfish reaches an internal temperature of at least 60 ºC on a meat thermometer. Serve immediately.

Crab Cakes

Prep time: 10 minutes | Cook time: 10 minutes | Serves 4

2 tins lump crab meat, 170 g each

¼ cup blanched finely ground almond flour

1 large egg

2 tablespoons full-fat mayonnaise

½ teaspoon Dijon mustard

½ tablespoon lemon juice

½ medium green pepper, seeded and chopped

235 g chopped spring onion

½ teaspoon Old Bay seasoning

1. In a large bowl, combine all ingredients. Form into four balls and flatten into patties. Place patties into the air fryer basket. 2. Adjust the temperature to 180ºC and air fry for 10 minutes. 3. Flip patties halfway through the cooking time. Serve warm.

Salmon Burgers with Creamy Broccoli Slaw

Prep time: 15 minutes | Cook time: 10 minutes | Serves 4

For The Salmon Burgers:

455 g salmon fillets, bones and skin removed

1 egg

10 g fresh dill, chopped

30 g fresh whole wheat bread crumbs

½ teaspoon salt

½ teaspoon cayenne pepper

2 garlic cloves, minced

4 whole wheat buns

For The Broccoli Slaw:

270 g chopped or shredded broccoli

25 g shredded carrots

30 g sunflower seeds

2 garlic cloves, minced

½ teaspoon salt

2 tablespoons apple cider vinegar

285 g nonfat plain Greek yoghurt

For The Salmon Burgers: 1. Preheat the air fryer to 180 ºC. 2. In a food processor, pulse the salmon fillets until they are finely chopped. 3. In a large bowl, combine the chopped salmon, egg, dill, bread crumbs, salt, cayenne, and garlic until it comes together. 4. Form the salmon into 4 patties. Place them into the air fryer basket, making sure that they don't touch each other. 5. Bake for 5 minutes. Flip the salmon patties and bake for 5 minutes more. For The Broccoli Slaw: 6. In a large bowl, combine all of the ingredients for the broccoli slaw. Mix well. 7. Serve the salmon burgers on toasted whole wheat buns, and top with a generous portion of broccoli slaw.

Prawns Curry

Prep time: 30 minutes | Cook time: 10 minutes | Serves 4

180 ml unsweetened full-fat coconut milk

10 g finely chopped brown onion

2 teaspoons garam masala

1 tablespoon minced fresh ginger

1 tablespoon minced garlic

1 teaspoon ground turmeric

1 teaspoon salt

¼ to ½ teaspoon cayenne pepper

455 g raw prawns (21 to 25 count), peeled and deveined

2 teaspoons chopped fresh coriander

1. In a large bowl, stir together the coconut milk, onion, garam masala, ginger, garlic, turmeric, salt and cayenne, until well blended. 2. Add the prawns and toss until coated with sauce on all sides. Marinate at room temperature for 30 minutes. 3. Transfer the prawns and marinade to a baking pan. Place the pan in the air fryer basket. Set the air fryer to 190°C for 10 minutes, stirring halfway through the cooking time. 4. Transfer the prawns to a serving bowl or platter. Sprinkle with the coriander and serve.

Seasoned Tuna Steaks

Prep time: 5 minutes | Cook time: 9 minutes | Serves 4

1 teaspoon garlic powder

½ teaspoon salt

¼ teaspoon dried thyme

¼ teaspoon dried oregano

4 tuna steaks

2 tablespoons olive oil

1 lemon, quartered

1. Preheat the air fryer to 190°C. 2. In a small bowl, whisk together the garlic powder, salt, thyme, and oregano. 3. Coat the tuna steaks with olive oil. Season both sides of each steak with the seasoning blend. Place the steaks in a single layer in the air fryer basket. 4. Roast for 5 minutes, then flip and roast for an additional 3 to 4 minutes.

Salmon with Fennel and Carrot

Prep time: 15 minutes | Cook time: 15 minutes | Serves 4

1 fennel bulb, thinly sliced

2 large carrots, sliced

1 large onion, thinly sliced

2 teaspoons extra-virgin olive oil

120 ml sour cream

1 teaspoon dried tarragon leaves

4 (140 g) salmon fillets

⅛ teaspoon salt

¼ teaspoon coarsely ground black pepper

1. Insert the crisper plate into the basket and the basket into the unit. Preheat the unit to 200°C, 2. In a medium bowl, toss together the fennel, carrots, and onion. Add the olive oil and toss again to coat the vegetables. Put

the vegetables into a 6-inch round metal pan. 3. Once the unit is preheated, place the pan into the basket. 4. Cook for 15 minutes. 5. Check after 5 minutes, the vegetables should be crisp-tender. Remove the pan and stir in the sour cream and tarragon. Top with the salmon fillets and sprinkle the fish with the salt and pepper. Reinsert the pan into the basket and resume cooking. 6. When the cooking is complete, the salmon should flake easily with a fork and a food thermometer should register at least 64°C. Serve the salmon on top of the vegetables.

Greek Fish Pitas

Prep time: 10 minutes | Cook time: 15 minutes | Serves 4

455 g pollock, cut into 1-inch pieces

60 ml olive oil

1 teaspoon salt

½ teaspoon dried oregano

½ teaspoon dried thyme

½ teaspoon garlic powder

¼ teaspoon cayenne

4 whole wheat pitas

75 g shredded lettuce

2 plum tomatoes, diced

Nonfat plain Greek yoghurt

Lemon, quartered

1. Preheat the air fryer to 190°C. 2. In a medium bowl, combine the pollock with olive oil, salt, oregano, thyme, garlic powder, and cayenne. 3. Put the pollock into the air fryer basket and roast for 15 minutes. 4. Serve inside pitas with lettuce, tomato, and Greek yoghurt with a lemon wedge on the side.

South Indian Fried Fish

Prep time: 20 minutes | Cook time: 8 minutes

| Serves 4

2 tablespoons olive oil

2 tablespoons fresh lime or lemon juice

1 teaspoon minced fresh ginger

1 clove garlic, minced

1 teaspoon ground turmeric

½ teaspoon kosher or coarse sea salt

¼ to ½ teaspoon cayenne pepper

455 g tilapia fillets (2 to 3 fillets)

Olive oil spray

Lime or lemon wedges (optional)

1. In a large bowl, combine the oil, lime juice, ginger, garlic, turmeric, salt, and cayenne. Stir until well combined; set aside. 2. Cut each tilapia fillet into three or four equal-size pieces. Add the fish to the bowl and gently mix until all of the fish is coated in the marinade. Marinate for 10 to 15 minutes at room temperature. (Don't marinate any longer or the acid in the lime juice will "cook" the fish.) 3. Spray the air fryer basket with olive oil spray. Place the fish in the basket and spray the fish. Set the air fryer to 160°C for 3 minutes to partially cook the fish. Set the air fryer to 200°C for 5 minutes to finish cooking and crisp up the fish. (Thinner pieces of fish will cook faster so you may want to check at the 3-minute mark of the second cooking time and remove those that are cooked through, and then add them back toward the end of the second cooking time to crisp.) 4. Carefully remove the fish from the basket. Serve hot, with lemon wedges if desired.

Lemon Mahi-Mahi

Prep time: 5 minutes | Cook time: 14 minutes | Serves 2

Olive or vegetable oil, for spraying

2 (170 g) dolphinfish

1 tablespoon lemon juice

1 tablespoon olive oil

¼ teaspoon salt

¼ teaspoon freshly ground black pepper

1 tablespoon chopped fresh dill

2 lemon slices

1. Line the air fryer basket with baking paper and spray lightly with oil. 2. Place the mahi-mahi in the prepared basket. 3. In a small bowl, whisk together the lemon juice and olive oil. Brush the mixture evenly over the mahi-mahi. 4. Sprinkle the mahi-mahi with the salt and black pepper and top with the dill. 5. Air fry at 200ºC for 12 to 14 minutes, depending on the thickness of the fillets, until they flake easily. 6. Transfer to plates, top each with a lemon slice, and serve.

Lemon-Tarragon Fish en Papillote

Prep time: 10 minutes | Cook time: 15 minutes | Serves 2

2 tablespoons salted butter, melted

1 tablespoon fresh lemon juice

½ teaspoon dried tarragon, crushed, or 2 sprigs fresh tarragon

1 teaspoon kosher or coarse sea salt

85 g julienned carrots

435 g julienned fennel, or 1 stalk julienned celery

75 g thinly sliced red pepper

2 cod fillets, 170 g each, thawed if frozen

Vegetable oil spray

½ teaspoon black pepper

1. In a medium bowl, combine the butter, lemon juice, tarragon, and ½ teaspoon of the salt. Whisk well until you get a creamy sauce. Add the carrots, fennel, and

pepper and toss to combine; set aside. 2. Cut two squares of baking paper each large enough to hold one fillet and half the vegetables. Spray the fillets with vegetable oil spray. Season both sides with the remaining ½ teaspoon salt and the black pepper. 3. Lay one fillet down on each baking paper square. Top each with half the vegetables. Pour any remaining sauce over the vegetables. 4. Fold over the baking paper and crimp the sides in small, tight folds to hold the fish, vegetables, and sauce securely inside the packet. Place the packets in the air fryer basket. Set the air fryer to 180 ºC for 15 minutes. 5. Transfer each packet to a plate. Cut open with scissors just before serving (be careful, as the steam inside will be hot).

Scallops with Asparagus and Peas

Prep time: 10 minutes | Cook time: 7 to 10 minutes | Serves 4

Cooking oil spray

455 g asparagus, ends trimmed, cut into 2-inch pieces

100 g sugar snap peas

455 g sea scallops

1 tablespoon freshly squeezed lemon juice

2 teaspoons extra-virgin olive oil

½ teaspoon dried thyme

Salt and freshly ground black pepper, to taste

1. Insert the crisper plate into the basket and the basket into the unit. Preheat the unit to 200 ºC. 2. Once the unit is preheated, spray the crisper plate with cooking oil. Place the asparagus and sugar snap peas into the basket. 3. Cook for 10 minutes. 4. Meanwhile, check the scallops for a small muscle attached to the side. Pull it off and discard. In a medium bowl, toss together the scallops, lemon juice, olive oil, and thyme. Season with salt and pepper. 5. After 3 minutes, the vegetables should be just starting to get tender. Place the scallops on top of the vegetables. Reinsert the basket to resume

cooking. After 3 minutes more, remove the basket and shake it. Again reinsert the basket to resume cooking. 6. When the cooking is complete, the scallops should be firm when tested with your finger and opaque in the center, and the vegetables tender. Serve immediately.

Paprika Crab Burgers

Prep time: 30 minutes | Cook time: 14 minutes | Serves 3

2 eggs, beaten

1 shallot, chopped

2 garlic cloves, crushed

1 tablespoon olive oil

1 teaspoon yellow mustard

1 teaspoon fresh coriander, chopped

280 g crab meat

1 teaspoon smoked paprika

½ teaspoon ground black pepper

Sea salt, to taste

70 g Parmesan cheese

1. In a mixing bowl, thoroughly combine the eggs, shallot, garlic, olive oil, mustard, coriander, crab meat, paprika, black pepper, and salt. Mix until well combined. 2. Shape the mixture into 6 patties. Roll the crab patties over grated Parmesan cheese, coating well on all sides. Place in your refrigerator for 2 hours. 3. Spritz the crab patties with cooking oil on both sides. Cook in the preheated air fryer at 180ºC for 14 minutes. Serve on bread rolls if desired. Bon appétit!

Tex-Mex Salmon Bowl

Prep time: 15 minutes | Cook time: 9 to 14 minutes | Serves 4

340 g salmon fillets, cut into 1½-inch cubes

1 red onion, chopped

1 red chilli, minced

1 red pepper, chopped

60 ml salsa

2 teaspoons peanut or safflower oil

2 tablespoons tomato juice

1 teaspoon chilli powder

1. Preheat the air fryer to 190ºC. 2. Mix together the salmon cubes, red onion, jalapeño, red pepper, salsa, peanut oil, tomato juice, chilli powder in a medium metal bowl and stir until well incorporated. 3. Transfer the bowl to the air fryer basket and bake for 9 to 14 minutes, stirring once, or until the salmon is cooked through and the veggies are fork-tender. 4. Serve warm.

Parmesan-Crusted Halibut Fillets

Prep time: 5 minutes | Cook time: 10 minutes | Serves 4

2 medium-sized halibut fillets

Dash of tabasco sauce

1 teaspoon curry powder

½ teaspoon ground coriander

½ teaspoon hot paprika

Kosher or coarse sea salt, and freshly cracked mixed peppercorns, to taste

2 eggs

1½ tablespoons olive oil

75 g grated Parmesan cheese

1. Preheat the air fryer to 190ºC. 2. On a clean work surface, drizzle the halibut fillets with the tabasco sauce. Sprinkle with the curry powder, coriander, hot paprika, salt, and cracked mixed peppercorns. Set aside. 3. In a shallow bowl, beat the eggs until frothy. In another shallow bowl, combine the olive oil and Parmesan cheese. 4. One at a time, dredge the halibut

fillits in the beaten eggs, shaking off any excess, then roll them over the Parmesan cheese until evenly coated. 5. Arrange the halibut fillets in the air fryer basket in a single layer and air fry for 10 minutes, or until the fish is golden brown and crisp. 6. Cool for 5 minutes before serving.

Lemon Pepper Prawns

Prep time: 15 minutes | Cook time: 8 minutes | Serves 2

Olive or vegetable oil, for spraying

340 g medium raw prawns, peeled and deveined

3 tablespoons lemon juice

1 tablespoon olive oil

1 teaspoon lemon pepper

¼ teaspoon paprika

¼ teaspoon granulated garlic

1. Preheat the air fryer to 200°C. Line the air fryer basket with baking paper and spray lightly with oil. 2. In a medium bowl, toss together the prawns, lemon juice, olive oil, lemon pepper, paprika, and garlic until evenly coated. 3. Place the prawns in the prepared basket. 4. Cook for 6 to 8 minutes, or until pink and firm. Serve immediately.

Crispy Fish Fingers

Prep time: 15 minutes | Cook time: 10 minutes | Serves 4

20 g crushed panko breadcrumbs

20 g blanched finely ground almond flour

½ teaspoon Old Bay seasoning

1 tablespoon coconut oil

1 large egg

455 g cod fillet, cut into ¾-inch strips

1. Place panko, almond flour, Old Bay seasoning, and

coconut oil into a large bowl and mix together. In a medium bowl, whisk egg. 2. Dip each fish stick into the egg and then gently press into the flour mixture, coating as fully and evenly as possible. Place fish fingers into the air fryer basket. 3. Adjust the temperature to 200ºC and air fry for 10 minutes or until golden. 4. Serve immediately.

Tuna Avocado Bites

Prep time: 10 minutes | Cook time: 7 minutes | Makes 12 bites

280 g canned tuna, drained

60 ml full-fat mayonnaise

1 stalk celery, chopped

1 medium avocado, peeled, pitted, and mashed

25 g blanched finely ground almond flour, divided

2 teaspoons coconut oil

1. In a large bowl, mix tuna, mayonnaise, celery, and mashed avocado. Form the mixture into balls. 2. Roll balls in almond flour and spritz with coconut oil. Place balls into the air fryer basket. 3. Adjust the temperature to 200ºC and set the timer for 7 minutes. 4. Gently turn tuna bites after 5 minutes. Serve warm.

Firecracker Prawns

Prep time: 10 minutes | Cook time: 7 minutes | Serves 4

455 g medium prawns, peeled and deveined

2 tablespoons salted butter, melted

½ teaspoon Old Bay seasoning

¼ teaspoon garlic powder

2 tablespoons Sriracha

¼ teaspoon powdered sweetener

60 ml full-fat mayonnaise

⅛ teaspoon ground black pepper

1. In a large bowl, toss prawns in butter, Old Bay seasoning, and garlic powder. Place prawns into the air fryer basket. 2. Adjust the temperature to 200ºC and set the timer for 7 minutes. 3. Flip the prawns halfway through the cooking time. Prawns will be bright pink when fully cooked. 4. In another large bowl, mix Sriracha, sweetener, mayonnaise, and pepper. Toss prawns in the spicy mixture and serve immediately.

Roasted Fish with Almond-Lemon Crumbs

Prep time: 10 minutes | Cook time: 7 to 8 minutes | Serves 4

70 g raw whole almonds

1 spring onion, finely chopped

Grated zest and juice of 1 lemon

½ tablespoon extra-virgin olive oil

¾ teaspoon kosher or coarse sea salt, divided

Freshly ground black pepper, to taste

4 skinless fish fillets, 170 g each

Cooking spray

1 teaspoon Dijon mustard

1. In a food processor, pulse the almonds to coarsely chop. Transfer to a small bowl and add the scallion, lemon zest, and olive oil. Season with ¼ teaspoon of the salt and pepper to taste and mix to combine. 2. Spray the top of the fish with oil and squeeze the lemon juice over the fish. Season with the remaining ½ teaspoon salt and pepper to taste. Spread the mustard on top of the fish. Dividing evenly, press the almond mixture onto the top of the fillets to adhere. 3. Preheat the air fryer to 190ºC. 4. Working in batches, place the fillets in the air fryer basket in a single layer. Air fry for 7 to 8 minutes, until the crumbs start to brown and the fish is cooked through. 5. Serve immediately.

Cajun and Lemon Pepper Cod

Prep time: 5 minutes | Cook time: 12 minutes | Makes 2 cod fillets

1 tablespoon Cajun seasoning

1 teaspoon salt

½ teaspoon lemon pepper

½ teaspoon freshly ground black pepper

2 cod fillets, 230 g each, cut to fit into the air fryer basket

Cooking spray

2 tablespoons unsalted butter, melted

1 lemon, cut into 4 wedges

1. Preheat the air fryer to 180°C. Spritz the air fryer basket with cooking spray. 2. Thoroughly combine the Cajun seasoning, salt, lemon pepper, and black pepper in a small bowl. Rub this mixture all over the cod fillets until completely coated. 3. Put the fillets in the air fryer basket and brush the melted butter over both sides of each fillet. 4. Bake in the preheated air fryer for 12 minutes, flipping the fillets halfway through, or until the fish flakes easily with a fork. 5. Remove the fillets from the basket and serve with fresh lemon wedges.

Fried Prawns

Prep time: 15 minutes | Cook time: 5 minutes | Serves 4

35 g self-raising flour

1 teaspoon paprika

1 teaspoon salt

½ teaspoon freshly ground black pepper

1 large egg, beaten

60 g finely crushed panko bread crumbs

20 frozen large prawns (about 900 g), peeled and

deveined

Cooking spray

1. In a shallow bowl, whisk the flour, paprika, salt, and pepper until blended. Add the beaten egg to a second shallow bowl and the bread crumbs to a third. 2. One at a time, dip the prawns into the flour, the egg, and the bread crumbs, coating thoroughly. 3. Preheat the air fryer to 200°C. Line the air fryer basket with baking paper. 4. Place the prawns on the baking paper and spritz with oil. 5. Air fry for 2 minutes. Shake the basket, spritz the prawns with oil, and air fry for 3 minutes more until lightly browned and crispy. Serve hot.

Moroccan Spiced Halibut with Chickpea Salad

Prep time: 15 minutes | Cook time: 12 minutes | Serves 2

¾ teaspoon ground coriander

½ teaspoon ground cumin

¼ teaspoon ground ginger

⅛ teaspoon ground cinnamon

Salt and pepper, to taste

2 (230 g) skinless halibut fillets, 1¼ inches thick

4 teaspoons extra-virgin olive oil, divided, plus extra for drizzling

425 g tin chickpeas, rinsed

1 tablespoon lemon juice, plus lemon wedges for serving

1 teaspoon harissa

½ teaspoon honey

2 carrots, peeled and shredded

2 tablespoons chopped fresh mint, divided

Vegetable oil spray

1. Preheat the air fryer to 150ºC. 2. Make foil sling for air fryer basket by folding 1 long sheet of aluminium foil so it is 4 inches wide. Lay sheet of foil widthwise across basket, pressing foil into and up sides of basket. Fold excess foil as needed so that edges of foil are flush with top of basket. Lightly spray foil and basket with vegetable oil spray. 3. Combine coriander, cumin, ginger, cinnamon, ⅛ teaspoon salt, and ⅛ teaspoon pepper in a small bowl. Pat halibut dry with paper towels, rub with 1 teaspoon oil, and sprinkle all over with spice mixture. Arrange fillets skinned side down on sling in prepared basket, spaced evenly apart. Bake until halibut flakes apart when gently prodded with a paring knife and registers 60 °C, 12 to 16 minutes, using the sling to rotate fillets halfway through cooking. 4. Meanwhile, microwave chickpeas in medium bowl until heated through, about 2 minutes. Stir in remaining 1 tablespoon oil, lemon juice, harissa, honey, ⅛ teaspoon salt, and ⅛ teaspoon pepper. Add carrots and 1 tablespoon mint and toss to combine. Season with salt and pepper, to taste. 5. Using sling, carefully remove halibut from air fryer and transfer to individual plates. Sprinkle with remaining 1 tablespoon mint and drizzle with extra oil to taste. Serve with salad and lemon wedges.

Roasted Cod with Lemon-Garlic Potatoes

Prep time: 10 minutes | Cook time: 28 minutes | Serves 2

3 tablespoons unsalted butter, softened, divided

2 garlic cloves, minced

1 lemon, grated to yield 2 teaspoons zest and sliced ¼ inch thick

Salt and pepper, to taste

1 large russet potato (about 340 g), unpeeled, sliced ¼ inch thick

1 tablespoon minced fresh parsley, chives, or

tarragon

2 (230 g) skinless cod fillets, 1¼ inches thick

Vegetable oil spray

1. Preheat the air fryer to 200°C. 2. Make foil sling for air fryer basket by folding 1 long sheet of aluminium foil so it is 4 inches wide. Lay sheet of foil widthwise across basket, pressing foil into and up sides of basket. Fold excess foil as needed so that edges of foil are flush with top of basket. Lightly spray the foil and basket with vegetable oil spray. 3. Microwave 1 tablespoon butter, garlic, 1 teaspoon lemon zest, ¼ teaspoon salt, and ⅛ teaspoon pepper in a medium bowl, stirring once, until the butter is melted and the mixture is fragrant, about 30 seconds. Add the potato slices and toss to coat. Shingle the potato slices on sling in prepared basket to create 2 even layers. Air fry until potato slices are spotty brown and just tender, 16 to 18 minutes, using a sling to rotate potatoes halfway through cooking. 4. Combine the remaining 2 tablespoons butter, remaining 1 teaspoon lemon zest, and parsley in a small bowl. Pat the cod dry with paper towels and season with salt and pepper. Place the fillets, skinned-side down, on top of potato slices, spaced evenly apart. (Tuck thinner tail ends of fillets under themselves as needed to create uniform pieces.) Dot the fillets with the butter mixture and top with the lemon slices. Return the basket to the air fryer and air fry until the cod flakes apart when gently prodded with a paring knife and registers 60°C, 12 to 15 minutes, using a sling to rotate the potato slices and cod halfway through cooking. 5. Using a sling, carefully remove potatoes and cod from air fryer. Cut the potato slices into 2 portions between fillets using fish spatula. Slide spatula along underside of potato slices and transfer with cod to individual plates. Serve.

Paprika Prawns

Prep time: 5 minutes | Cook time: 6 minutes | Serves 2

230 g medium prawns, peeled and deveined

2 tablespoons salted butter, melted

1 teaspoon paprika

½ teaspoon garlic powder

¼ teaspoon onion powder

½ teaspoon Old Bay seasoning

1. Toss all ingredients together in a large bowl. Place prawns into the air fryer basket. 2. Adjust the temperature to 200°C and set the timer for 6 minutes. 3. Turn the prawns halfway through the cooking time to ensure even cooking. Serve immediately.

Catfish Bites

Prep time: 15 minutes | Cook time: 20 minutes | Serves 4

Olive or vegetable oil, for spraying

455 g catfish fillets, cut into 2-inch pieces

235 ml buttermilk

35 g cornmeal

20 g plain flour

2 teaspoons Creole seasoning

120 ml yellow mustard

1. Line the air fryer basket with baking paper and spray lightly with oil. 2. Place the catfish pieces and buttermilk in a zip-top plastic bag, seal, and refrigerate for about 10 minutes. 3. In a shallow bowl, mix together the cornmeal, flour, and Creole seasoning. 4. Remove the catfish from the bag and pat dry with a paper towel. 5. Spread the mustard on all sides of the catfish, then dip them in the cornmeal mixture until evenly coated. 6. Place the catfish in the prepared basket. You may need to work in batches, depending on the size of your air fryer. Spray lightly with oil. 7. Air fry at 200°C for 10 minutes, flip carefully, spray with oil, and cook for another 10 minutes. Serve immediately.

Black Cod with Grapes and Kale

Prep time: 10 minutes | Cook time: 15 minutes | Serves 2

2 fillets of black cod, 200 g each

Salt and freshly ground black pepper, to taste

Olive oil

150 g grapes, halved

1 small bulb fennel, sliced ¼-inch thick

65 g pecans

200 g shredded kale

2 teaspoons white balsamic vinegar or white wine vinegar

2 tablespoons extra-virgin olive oil

1. Preheat the air fryer to 200°C. 2. Season the cod fillets with salt and pepper and drizzle, brush or spray a little olive oil on top. Place the fish, presentation side up (skin side down), into the air fryer basket. Air fry for 10 minutes. 3. When the fish has finished cooking, remove the fillets to a side plate and loosely tent with foil to rest. 4. Toss the grapes, fennel and pecans in a bowl with a drizzle of olive oil and season with salt and pepper. Add the grapes, fennel and pecans to the air fryer basket and air fry for 5 minutes, shaking the basket once during the cooking time. 5. Transfer the grapes, fennel and pecans to a bowl with the kale. Dress the kale with the balsamic vinegar and olive oil, season to taste with salt and pepper and serve alongside the cooked fish.

Sea Bass with Potato Scales

Prep time: 10 minutes | Cook time: 10 minutes | Serves 2

2 fillets of sea bass, 170- to 230 g each

Salt and freshly ground black pepper, to taste

60 ml mayonnaise

2 teaspoons finely chopped lemon zest

1 teaspoon chopped fresh thyme

2 Fingerling, or new potatoes, very thinly sliced into rounds

Olive oil

½ clove garlic, crushed into a paste

1 tablespoon capers, drained and rinsed

1 tablespoon olive oil

1 teaspoon lemon juice, to taste

1. Preheat the air fryer to 200°C. 2. Season the fish well with salt and freshly ground black pepper. Mix the mayonnaise, lemon zest and thyme together in a small bowl. Spread a thin layer of the mayonnaise mixture on both fillets. Start layering rows of potato slices onto the fish fillets to simulate the fish scales. The second row should overlap the first row slightly. Dabbing a little more mayonnaise along the upper edge of the row of potatoes where the next row overlaps will help the potato slices stick. Press the potatoes onto the fish to secure them well and season again with salt. Brush or spray the potato layer with olive oil. 3. Transfer the fish to the air fryer and air fry for 8 to 10 minutes, depending on the thickness of your fillets. 1-inch of fish should take 10 minutes at 200ºC. 4. While the fish is cooking, add the garlic, capers, olive oil and lemon juice to the remaining mayonnaise mixture to make the caper aïoli. 5. Serve the fish warm with a dollop of the aïoli on top or on the side.

Chapter 7 Snacks and Starters

Cheesy Courgette Tots

Prep time: 15 minutes | Cook time: 6 minutes | Serves 8

2 medium courgette (about 340 g), shredded

1 large egg, whisked

72 g grated pecorino Romano cheese

42 g panko breadcrumbs

¼ teaspoon black pepper

1 clove garlic, minced

Cooking spray

1. Using your hands, squeeze out as much liquid from the courgette as possible. In a large bowl, mix the courgette with the remaining ingredients except the oil until well incorporated. 2. Make the courgette tots: Use a spoon or biscuit scoop to place tablespoonfuls of the courgette mixture onto a lightly floured cutting board and form into 1-inch logs. 3. Preheat air fryer to 190ºC. Spritz the air fryer basket with cooking spray. 4. Place the tots in the basket. You may need to cook in batches to avoid overcrowding. 5. Air fry for 6 minutes until golden. 6. Remove from the basket to a serving plate and repeat with the remaining courgette tots. 7. Serve immediately.

Goat Cheese and Garlic Crostini

Prep time: 3 minutes | Cook time: 5 minutes | Serves 4

1 wholemeal baguette

60 ml olive oil

2 garlic cloves, minced

113 g goat cheese

2 tablespoons fresh basil, minced

1. Preheat the air fryer to 190ºC. 2. Cut the baguette into ½-inch-thick slices. 3. In a small bowl, mix together the olive oil and garlic, then brush it over one side of each slice of bread. 4. Place the olive-oil-coated bread in a single layer in the air fryer basket and bake for 5 minutes. 5. Meanwhile, in a small bowl, mix together the goat cheese and basil. 6. Remove the toast from the air fryer, then spread a thin layer of the goat cheese mixture over the top of each piece and serve.

Kale Crisps with Sesame

Prep time: 15 minutes | Cook time: 8 minutes | Serves 5

2L deribbed kale leaves, torn into 2-inch pieces

1½ tablespoons olive oil

¾ teaspoon chilli powder

¼ teaspoon garlic powder

½ teaspoon paprika

2 teaspoons sesame seeds

1. Preheat air fryer to 180ºC. 2. In a large bowl, toss the kale with the olive oil, chilli powder, garlic powder, paprika, and sesame seeds until well coated. 3. Put the kale in the air fryer basket and air fry for 8 minutes, flipping the kale twice during cooking, or until the kale is crispy. 4. Serve warm.

Veggie Salmon Nachos

Prep time: 10 minutes | Cook time: 9 to 12 minutes | Serves 6

57 g baked no-salt sweetcorn tortilla chips

1 (142 g) baked salmon fillet, flaked

100 g canned low-salt black beans, rinsed and drained

1 red pepper, chopped

50 g grated carrot

1 jalapeño chillies pepper, minced

30 g shredded low-salt low-fat Swiss cheese

1 tomato, chopped

1. Preheat the air fryer to 180°C. 2. In a baking pan, layer the tortilla chips. Top with the salmon, black beans, red pepper, carrot, jalapeño chillies, and Swiss cheese. 3. Bake in the air fryer for 9 to 12 minutes, or until the cheese is melted and starts to brown. 4. Top with the tomato and serve.

Golden Salmon and Carrot Croquettes

Prep time: 15 minutes | Cook time: 10 minutes | Serves 6

2 egg whites

120 g almond flour

120 g panko breadcrumbs

450 g chopped salmon fillet

160 g grated carrots

2 tablespoons minced garlic cloves

120 g chopped onion

2 tablespoons chopped chives

Cooking spray

1. Preheat the air fryer to 180°C 2.Spritz the air fryer basket with cooking spray 3.Whisk the egg whites in a bowl 4.Put the flour in a second bowl 5.Pour the breadcrumbs in a third bowl 6.Set aside 7.Combine the salmon, carrots, garlic, onion, and chives in a large bowl 8.Stir to mix well 9.Form the mixture into balls with your hands 10.Dredge the balls into the flour, then egg, and then breadcrumbs to coat well 11.Arrange the salmon balls in the preheated air fryer and spritz with cooking spray 12.Air fry for 10 minutes or until crispy and browned 13.Shake the basket halfway through 14.Serve immediately.

Lebanese Muhammara

Prep time: 15 minutes | Cook time: 15 minutes | Serves 6

2 large red peppers

60 ml plus 2 tablespoons extra-virgin olive oil

85 g walnut halves

1 tablespoon agave syrup or honey

1 teaspoon fresh lemon juice

1 teaspoon cumin powder

1 teaspoon rock salt

1 teaspoon red pepper flakes

Raw mixed vegetables (such as cucumber, carrots, sliced courgette, or cauliflower) or toasted pitta bread chips, for serving

1. Drizzle the peppers with 2 tablespoons of the olive oil and place in the air fryer basket. Set the air fryer to 200ºC for 10 minutes. 2. Add the walnuts to the basket, arranging them around the peppers. Set the air fryer to 200ºC for 5 minutes. 3. Remove the peppers, seal in a a resealable plastic bag, and let rest for 5 to 10 minutes. Transfer the walnuts to a plate and set aside to cool down. 4. Place the softened peppers, walnuts, agave, lemon juice, cumin, salt, and ½ teaspoon of the pepper flakes blend in a food processor until smooth. 5. Transfer the dip to a serving bowl and create an indentation in the middle. Pour the remaining 60 ml olive oil into the indentation. Garnish the dip with the remaining ½ teaspoon pepper flakes. 6. Serve with mixed vegetables or toasted pitta bread chips.

Lemony Pear Chips

Prep time: 15 minutes | Cook time: 9 to 13 minutes | Serves 4

2 firm Bosc or Anjou pears, cut crosswise into ⅛ -inch-thick slices

1 tablespoon freshly squeezed lemon juice

½ teaspoon cinnamon powder

⅛ teaspoon ground cardamom

1. Preheat the air fryer to 190 °C. 2. Separate the smaller stem-end pear rounds from the larger rounds with seeds. Remove the core and seeds from the larger slices. Sprinkle all slices with lemon juice, cinnamon, and cardamom. 3. Put the smaller crisps into the air fryer basket. Air fry for 3 to 5 minutes, or until light golden, shaking the basket once during cooking. Remove from the air fryer. 4. Repeat with the larger slices, air frying for 6 to 8 minutes, or until light golden, shaking the basket once during cooking. 5. Remove the crisps from the air fryer. Cool and serve or store in an airtight container at room temperature up for to 2 days.

Greek Potato Skins with Olives and Feta

Prep time: 5 minutes | Cook time: 45 minutes | Serves 4

2 russet potatoes or Maris Piper potatoes

3 tablespoons olive oil, divided, plus more for drizzling (optional)

1 teaspoon rock salt, divided

¼ teaspoon black pepper

2 tablespoons fresh coriander, chopped, plus more for serving

60 g Kalamata olives, diced

60 g crumbled feta cheese

Chopped fresh parsley, for garnish (optional)

1. Preheat the air fryer to 190°C. 2. Using a fork, poke 2 to 3 holes in the potatoes, then coat each with about ½ tablespoon olive oil and ½ teaspoon salt. 3. Place the potatoes into the air fryer basket and bake for 30 minutes. 4. Remove the potatoes from the air fryer, and slice in half. Using a spoon, scoop out the flesh of the potatoes, leaving a ½-inch layer of potato inside the skins, and set the skins aside. 5. In a medium-sized bowl, combine the scooped potato middles with the remaining 2 tablespoons of olive oil, ½ teaspoon of salt, black pepper, and coriander. Mix until well combined. 6. Divide the potato filling into the now-empty potato skins, spreading it evenly over them. Top each potato with a tablespoon each of the olives and feta cheese. 7. Place the loaded potato skins back into the air fryer and bake for 15 minutes. 8. Serve with additional chopped coriander or parsley and a drizzle of olive oil, if desired.

Egg Roll Pizza Sticks

Prep time: 10 minutes | Cook time: 5 minutes | Serves 4

Olive oil

8 pieces low-fat string cheese

8 egg roll wrappers or spring roll pastry

24 slices turkey pepperoni or salami

Marinara sauce, for dipping (optional)

1. Spray the air fryer basket lightly with olive oil. Fill a small bowl with water. 2. Place each egg roll wrapper diagonally on a work surface. It should look like a diamond. 3. Place 3 slices of turkey pepperoni in a vertical line down the centre of the wrapper. 4. Place 1 mozzarella cheese cheese stick on top of the turkey pepperoni. 5. Fold the top and bottom corners of the egg roll wrapper over the cheese stick. 6. Fold the left corner over the cheese stick and roll the cheese stick up to resemble a spring roll. Dip a finger in the water and seal the edge of the roll 7. Repeat with the rest of the pizza sticks. 8. Place them in the air fryer basket in a single layer, making sure to leave a little space between each one. Lightly spray the pizza sticks with oil. You may need to cook these in batches. 9. Air fry at 190 °C until the pizza sticks are lightly browned and crispy, about 5 minutes. 10. These are best served hot while the cheese is melted. Accompany with a small bowl of marinara sauce, if desired.

Crispy Chilli Chickpeas

Prep time: 5 minutes | Cook time: 15 minutes | Serves 4

1 (425 g) tin cooked chickpeas, drained and rinsed

1 tablespoon olive oil

¼ teaspoon salt

⅛ teaspoon chilli powder

⅛ teaspoon garlic powder

⅛ teaspoon paprika

1. Preheat the air fryer to 190°C. 2. In a medium-sized bowl, toss all of the ingredients together until the chickpeas are well coated. 3. Pour the chickpeas into the air fryer and spread them out in a single layer. 4. Roast for 15 minutes, stirring once halfway through the cook time.

Sea Salt Potato Crisps

Prep time: 30 minutes | Cook time: 27 minutes | Serves 4

Oil, for spraying

4 medium-sized yellow potatoes such as Maris Piper potatoes

1 tablespoon oil

⅛ to ¼ teaspoon fine sea salt

1. Line the air fryer basket with baking paper and spray lightly with oil. 2. Using a mandoline or a very sharp knife, cut the potatoes into very thin slices. 3. Place the slices in a bowl of cold water and let soak for about 20 minutes. 4. Drain the potatoes, transfer them to a plate lined with kitchen roll, and pat dry. 5. Drizzle the oil over the potatoes, sprinkle with the salt, and toss to combine. Transfer to the prepared basket. 6. Air fry at 90°C for 20 minutes. Toss the crisps, increase the heat to 200°C, and cook for another 5 to 7 minutes, until crispy.

Golden Onion Rings

Prep time: 15 minutes | Cook time: 14 minutes per batch | Serves 4

1 large white onion, peeled and cut into ½ to ¾ -inch-thick slices (about 475 g)

120 ml semi-skimmed milk

115 g wholemeal pastry flour, or plain flour

2 tablespoons cornflour

¾ teaspoon sea salt, divided

½ teaspoon freshly ground black pepper, divided

¾ teaspoon garlic powder, divided

110 g wholemeal breadcrumbs, or gluten-free breadcrumbs

Cooking oil spray (coconut, sunflower, or safflower)

tomato ketchup, for serving (optional)

1. Carefully separate the onion slices into rings — a gentle touch is important here. 2. Place the milk in a shallow dish and set aside. 3. Make the first breading: In a medium-sized bowl, stir together the flour, cornflour, ¼ teaspoon of salt, ¼ teaspoon of pepper, and ¼ teaspoon of garlic powder. Set aside. 4. Make the second breading: In a separate medium bowl, stir together the breadcrumbs with the remaining ½ teaspoon of salt, the remaining ½ teaspoon of garlic, and the remaining ½ teaspoon of pepper. Set aside. 5. Insert the crisper plate into the basket and the basket into the unit. Preheat the unit by selecting AIR FRY, setting the temperature to 200°C, and setting the time to 3 minutes. Select START/STOP to begin. 6. Once the unit is preheated, spray the crisper plate and the basket with cooking oil. 7. To make the onion rings, dip one ring into the milk and into the first breading mixture. Dip the ring into the milk again and back into the first breading mixture, coating thoroughly. Dip the ring into the milk one last time and then into the second breading mixture, coating thoroughly. Gently

lay the onion ring in the basket. Repeat with additional rings and, as you place them into the basket, do not overlap them too much. Once all the onion rings are in the basket, generously spray the tops with cooking oil. 8. Select AIR FRY, set the temperature to 200°C, and set the time to 14 minutes. Insert the basket into the unit. Select START/STOP to begin. 9. After 4 minutes, open the unit and spray the rings generously with cooking oil. Close the unit to resume cooking. After 3 minutes, remove the basket and spray the onion rings again. Remove the rings, turn them over, and place them back into the basket. Generously spray them again with oil. Reinsert the basket to resume cooking. After 4 minutes, generously spray the rings with oil one last time. Resume cooking for the remaining 3 minutes, or until the onion rings are very crunchy and brown. 10. When the cooking is complete, serve the hot rings with tomato ketchup, or other sauce of choice.

Cheese-Stuffed Blooming Onion

Prep time: 10 minutes | Cook time: 15 minutes | Serves 2

1 large brown onion (397 g)

1 tablespoon olive oil

Rock salt and freshly ground black pepper, to taste

18 g plus 2 tablespoons panko breadcrumbs

22 g grated Parmesan cheese

3 tablespoons mayonnaise

1 tablespoon fresh lemon juice

1 tablespoon chopped fresh flat-leaf parsley parsley

2 teaspoons wholemeal Dijon mustard

1 garlic clove, minced

1. Place the onion on a cutting board and trim the top off and peel off the outer skin. Turn the onion upside down and use a paring knife, cut vertical slits halfway through the onion at ½-inch intervals around the onion, keeping the root intact. When you turn the onion right side up, it should open up like the petals of a flower. Drizzle the cut sides of the onion with the olive oil and season with salt and pepper. Place petal-side up in the air fryer and air fry at 180°C for 10 minutes. 2. Meanwhile, in a bowl, stir together the panko, Parmesan, mayonnaise, lemon juice, parsley, mustard, and garlic until incorporated into a smooth paste. 3. Remove the onion from the fryer and stuff the paste all over and in between the onion "petals." Return the onion to the air fryer and air fry at 190°C until the onion is tender in the centre and the bread crumb mixture is golden, about 5 minutes. Remove the onion from the air fryer, transfer to a plate, and serve hot.

Poutine with Waffle Fries

Prep time: 10 minutes | Cook time: 15 to 17 minutes | Serves 4

225 g frozen waffle cut fries

2 teaspoons olive oil

1 red pepper, chopped

2 spring onions, sliced

90 g shredded Swiss cheese

120 ml bottled chicken gravy

1. Preheat the air fryer to 190°C. 2. Toss the waffle fries with the olive oil and place in the air fryer basket. Air fry for 10 to 12 minutes, or until the fries are crisp and light golden, shaking the basket halfway through the cooking time. 3. Transfer the fries to a baking pan and top with the pepper, spring onions, and cheese. Air fry for 3 minutes, or until the mixed vegetables are crisp and tender. 4. Remove the pan from the air fryer and drizzle the gravy over the fries. Air fry for 2 minutes, or until the gravy is hot. 5. Serve immediately.

Supplì al Telefono (Risotto Croquettes)

Prep time: 1 hour 40 minutes | Cook time: 1 hour | Serves 6

Risotto Croquettes:

4 tablespoons unsalted butter

1 small brown onion, minced

235 g Arborio rice

820 g chicken stock

120 g dry white wine

3 eggs

Zest of 1 lemon

120 g grated Parmesan cheese

60 g fresh Mozzarella cheese

60 g peas

2 tablespoons water

60 g plain flour

175 g panko breadcrumbs

Rock salt and ground black pepper, to taste

Cooking spray

Tomato Sauce:

2 tablespoons extra-virgin olive oil

4 cloves garlic, minced

¼ teaspoon red pepper flakes

1 (794 g) can crushed tomatoes or passata

2 teaspoons granulated sugar

Rock salt and ground black pepper, to taste

1. Melt the butter in a pot over medium heat, then add the onion and salt to taste 2.Sauté for 5 minutes or until the onion is translucent 3.Add the rice and stir to coat well 4.Cook for 3 minutes or until the rice is lightly browned 5.Pour in the chicken stock and wine 6.Bring to a boil 7.Then cook for 20 minutes or until the rice is tender and liquid is almost absorbed 8.Make the risotto: When the rice is cooked, break the egg into the pot 9.Add the lemon zest and Parmesan cheese 10.Sprinkle with salt and ground black pepper 11.Stir to mix well 12.Pour the risotto in a baking sheet, then level with a spatula to spread the risotto evenly 13.Wrap the baking sheet in plastic and refrigerate for1 hour 14.Meanwhile, heat the olive oil in a saucepan over medium heat until shimmering 15.Add the garlic and sprinkle with red pepper flakes 16.Sauté for a minute or until fragrant 17.Add the crushed tomatoes and sprinkle with sugar 18.Stir to mix well 19.Bring to a boil 20.Reduce the heat to low and simmer for 15 minutes or until lightly thickened 21.Sprinkle with salt and pepper to taste 22.Set aside until ready to serve 23.Remove the risotto from the refrigerator 24.Scoop the risotto into twelve 2-inch balls, then flatten the balls with your hands 25.Arrange a about ½-inch piece of Mozzarella and 5 peas in the centre of each flattened ball, then wrap them back into balls 26.Transfer the balls in a baking sheet lined with parchment paper, then refrigerate for 15 minutes or until firm 27.Preheat the air fryer to 200° C 28.Whisk the remaining 2 eggs with 2 tablespoons of water in a bowl 29.Pour the flour in a second bowl and pour the panko in a third bowl 30.Dredge the risotto balls in the bowl of flour first, then into the eggs, and then into the panko 31.Shake the excess off 32.Transfer the balls in the preheated air fryer and spritz with cooking spray 33.You may need to work in batches to avoid overcrowding 34.Bake for 10 minutes or until golden brown 35.Flip the balls halfway through 36.Serve the risotto balls with the tomato sauce.

Greens Crisps with Curried Yoghurt Sauce

Prep time: 10 minutes | Cook time: 5 to 6 minutes | Serves 4

240 ml low-fat Greek yoghurt

1 tablespoon freshly squeezed lemon juice

1 tablespoon curry powder

½ bunch curly kale, stemmed, ribs removed and discarded, leaves cut into 2- to 3-inch pieces

½ bunch chard, stemmed, ribs removed and discarded, leaves cut into 2- to 3-inch pieces

1½ teaspoons olive oil

1. In a small bowl, stir together the yoghurt, lemon juice, and curry powder. Set aside. 2. In a large bowl, toss the kale and chard with the olive oil, working the oil into the leaves with your hands. This helps break up the fibres in the leaves so the crisps are tender. 3. Air fry the greens in batches at 200°C for 5 to 6 minutes, until crisp, shaking the basket once during cooking. Serve with the yoghurt sauce.

Pork and Cabbage Egg Rolls

Prep time: 15 minutes | Cook time: 12 minutes | Makes 12 egg rolls

Cooking oil spray

2 garlic cloves, minced

340 g minced pork

1 teaspoon sesame oil

60 ml soy sauce

2 teaspoons grated peeled fresh ginger

110 g shredded green cabbage

4 spring onions, green parts (white parts optional), chopped

24 egg roll wrappers

1. Spray a frying pan with the cooking oil and place it over medium-high heat. Add the garlic and cook for 1 minute until fragrant. 2. Add the minced pork to the frying pan. Using a spoon, break the pork into smaller chunks. 3. In a small bowl, whisk the sesame oil, soy sauce, and ginger until combined. Add the sauce to the frying pan. Stir to combine and continue cooking for about 5 minutes until the pork is browned and thoroughly cooked. 4. Stir in the cabbage and spring onions. Transfer the pork mixture to a large bowl. 5. Lay the egg roll wrappers on a flat surface. Dip a basting brush in water and glaze each egg roll wrapper along the edges with the wet brush. This will soften the dough and make it easier to roll. 6. Stack 2 egg roll wrappers (it works best if you double-wrap the egg rolls). Scoop 1 to 2 tablespoons of the pork mixture into the centre of each wrapper stack. 7. Roll one long side of the wrappers up over the filling. Press firmly on the area with the filling, tucking it in lightly to secure it in place. Fold in the left and right sides. Continue rolling to close. Use the basting brush to wet the seam and seal the egg roll. Repeat with the remaining ingredients. 8. Insert the crisper plate into the basket and the basket into the unit. Preheat the unit by selecting AIR FRY, setting the temperature to 200°C, and setting the time to 3 minutes. Select START/STOP to begin. 9. Once the unit is preheated, spray the crisper plate with cooking oil. Place the egg rolls into the basket. It is okay to stack them. Spray them with cooking oil. 10. Select AIR FRY, set the temperature to 200°C, and set the time to 12 minutes. Insert the basket into the unit. Select START/STOP to begin. 11. After 8 minutes, use tongs to flip the egg rolls. Reinsert the basket to resume cooking. 12. When the cooking is complete, serve the egg rolls hot.

Bruschetta with Basil Pesto

Prep time: 10 minutes | Cook time: 5 to 11 minutes | Serves 4

8 slices French bread, ½ inch thick

2 tablespoons softened butter

120 g shredded mozzarella cheese cheese

120 g basil pesto

240 g chopped cherry tomatoes

2 spring onions, thinly sliced

1. Preheat the air fryer to 180°C. 2. Spread the bread with the butter and place butter-side up in the air fryer basket. Bake for 3 to 5 minutes, or until the bread is light golden. 3. Remove the bread from the basket and top each piece with some of the cheese. Return to the basket in 2 batches and bake for 1 to 3 minutes, or until the cheese melts. 4. Meanwhile, combine the pesto, tomatoes, and spring onions in a small bowl. 5. When the cheese has melted, remove the bread from the air fryer and place on a serving plate. Top each slice with some of the pesto mixture and serve.

Garlic-Roasted Tomatoes and Olives

Prep time: 5 minutes | Cook time: 20 minutes | Serves 6

300 g cherry tomatoes

4 garlic cloves, roughly chopped

½ red onion, roughly chopped

160 g black olives

180 g green olives

1 tablespoon fresh basil, minced

1 tablespoon fresh oregano, minced

2 tablespoons olive oil

¼ to ½ teaspoon salt

1. Preheat the air fryer to 190°C. 2. In a large bowl, combine all of the ingredients and toss together so that the tomatoes and olives are coated well with the olive oil and herbs. 3. Pour the mixture into the air fryer basket, and roast for 10 minutes. Stir the mixture well, then continue roasting for an additional 10 minutes. 4. Remove from the air fryer, transfer to a serving bowl, and enjoy.

Grilled Gammon and Cheese on Raisin Bread

Prep time: 5 minutes | Cook time: 10 minutes | Serves 1

2 slices sultana bread or fruit loaf

2 tablespoons butter, softened

2 teaspoons honey mustard

3 slices thinly sliced honey roast gammon (about 85 g)

4 slices Muenster cheese (about 85 g)

2 cocktail sticks

1. Preheat the air fryer to 190°C. 2. Spread the softened butter on one side of both slices of bread and place the bread, buttered side down on the counter. Spread the honey mustard on the other side of each slice of bread. Layer 2 slices of cheese, the gammon and the remaining 2 slices of cheese on one slice of bread and top with the other slice of bread. Remember to leave the buttered side of the bread on the outside. 3. Transfer the sandwich to the air fryer basket and secure the sandwich with cocktail sticks. 4. Air fry for 5 minutes. Flip the sandwich over, remove the cocktail sticks and air fry for another 5 minutes. Cut the sandwich in half and enjoy!

Chapter 8 Vegetables and Sides

Garlic Roasted Broccoli

Prep time: 8 minutes | Cook time: 10 to 14 minutes | Serves 6

1 head broccoli, cut into bite-size florets

1 tablespoon avocado oil

2 teaspoons minced garlic

⅛ teaspoon red pepper flakes

Sea salt and freshly ground black pepper, to taste

1 tablespoon freshly squeezed lemon juice

½ teaspoon lemon zest

1. In a large bowl, toss together the broccoli, avocado oil, garlic, red pepper flakes, salt, and pepper. 2. Set the air fryer to 190°C. Arrange the broccoli in a single layer in the air fryer basket, working in batches if necessary. Roast for 10 to 14 minutes, until the broccoli is lightly charred. 3. Place the florets in a medium bowl and toss with the lemon juice and lemon zest. Serve.

Cauliflower Steaks Gratin

Prep time: 10 minutes | Cook time: 13 minutes | Serves 2

1 head cauliflower

1 tablespoon olive oil

Salt and freshly ground black pepper, to taste

½ teaspoon chopped fresh thyme leaves

3 tablespoons grated Parmigiano-Reggiano cheese

2 tablespoons panko bread crumbs

1. Preheat the air fryer to 190°C. 2. Cut two steaks out of the centre of the cauliflower. To do this, cut the cauliflower in half and then cut one slice about 1-inch thick off each half. The rest of the cauliflower will fall apart into florets, which you tin roast on their own or save for another meal. 3. Brush both sides of the cauliflower steaks with olive oil and season with salt, freshly ground black pepper and fresh thyme. Place the cauliflower steaks into the air fryer basket and air fry for 6 minutes. Turn the steaks over and air fry for another 4 minutes. Combine the Parmesan cheese and panko bread crumbs and sprinkle the mixture over the tops of both steaks and air fry for another 3 minutes until the cheese has melted and the bread crumbs have browned. Serve this with some sautéed bitter greens and air-fried blistered tomatoes.

Sesame Carrots and Sugar Snap Peas

Prep time: 10 minutes | Cook time: 16 minutes | Serves 4

450 g carrots, peeled sliced on the bias (½ -inch slices)

1 teaspoon olive oil

Salt and freshly ground black pepper, to taste

110 g honey

1 tablespoon sesame oil

1 tablespoon soy sauce

½ teaspoon minced fresh ginger

110 g sugar snap peas

1½ teaspoons sesame seeds

1. Preheat the air fryer to 180°C. 2. Toss the carrots with the olive oil, season with salt and pepper and air fry for 10 minutes, shaking the basket once or twice during the cooking process. 3. Combine the honey, sesame oil, soy sauce and minced ginger in a large bowl. Add the sugar snap peas and the air-fried carrots to the honey mixture, toss to coat and return everything to the air fryer basket. 4. Turn up the temperature to 200°C and air fry for an additional 6 minutes, shaking

the basket once during the cooking process. 5. Transfer the carrots and sugar snap peas to a serving bowl. Pour the sauce from the bottom of the cooker over the vegetables and sprinkle sesame seeds over top. Serve immediately.

Simple Air Fried Crispy Brussels Sprouts

Prep time: 5 minutes | Cook time: 20 minutes | Serves 4

¼ teaspoon salt

⅛ teaspoon ground black pepper

1 tablespoon extra-virgin olive oil

450 g Brussels sprouts, trimmed and halved

Lemon wedges, for garnish

1. Preheat the air fryer to 180°C 2.Combine the salt, black pepper, and olive oil in a large bowl 3.Stir to mix well 4.Add the Brussels sprouts to the bowl of mixture and toss to coat well 5.Arrange the Brussels sprouts in the preheated air fryer 6.Air fry for 20 minutes or until lightly browned and wilted 7.Shake the basket two times during the air frying 8.Transfer the cooked Brussels sprouts to a large plate and squeeze the lemon wedges on top to serve.

Saltine Wax Beans

Prep time: 10 minutes | Cook time: 7 minutes | Serves 4

60 g flour

1 teaspoon smoky chipotle powder

½ teaspoon ground black pepper

1 teaspoon sea salt flakes

2 eggs, beaten

55 g crushed cream crackers

285 g wax beans

Cooking spray

1. Preheat the air fryer to 180°C. 2. Combine the flour, chipotle powder, black pepper, and salt in a bowl. Put the eggs in a second bowl. Put the crushed cream crackers in a third bowl. 3. Wash the beans with cold water and discard any tough strings. 4. Coat the beans with the flour mixture, before dipping them into the beaten egg. Cover them with the crushed cream crackers. 5. Spritz the beans with cooking spray. 6. Air fry for 4 minutes. Give the air fryer basket a good shake and continue to air fry for 3 minutes. Serve hot.

Parmesan-Thyme Butternut Marrow

Prep time: 15 minutes | Cook time: 20 minutes | Serves 4

350 g butternut marrow, cubed into 1-inch pieces (approximately 1 medium)

2 tablespoons olive oil

¼ teaspoon salt

¼ teaspoon garlic powder

¼ teaspoon black pepper

1 tablespoon fresh thyme

20 g grated Parmesan

1. Preheat the air fryer to 180°C. 2. In a large bowl, combine the cubed marrow with the olive oil, salt, garlic powder, pepper, and thyme until the marrow is well coated. 3. Pour this mixture into the air fryer basket, and roast for 10 minutes. Stir and roast another 8 to 10 minutes more. 4. Remove the marrow from the air fryer and toss with freshly grated Parmesan before serving.

Zesty Fried Asparagus

Prep time: 3 minutes | Cook time: 10 minutes | Serves 4

Oil, for spraying

10 to 12 spears asparagus, trimmed

2 tablespoons olive oil

1 tablespoon garlic powder

1 teaspoon chilli powder

½ teaspoon ground cumin

¼ teaspoon salt

1. Line the air fryer basket with parchment and spray lightly with oil. 2. If the asparagus are too long to fit easily in the air fryer, cut them in half. 3. Place the asparagus, olive oil, garlic, chilli powder, cumin, and salt in a zip-top plastic bag, seal, and toss until evenly coated. 4. Place the asparagus in the prepared basket. 5. Roast at 200 °C for 5 minutes, flip, and cook for another 5 minutes, or until bright green and firm but tender.

Butternut Marrow Croquettes

Prep time: 5 minutes | Cook time: 17 minutes | Serves 4

⅓ butternut marrow, peeled and grated

40 g plain flour

2 eggs, whisked

4 cloves garlic, minced

1½ tablespoons olive oil

1 teaspoon fine sea salt

⅓ teaspoon freshly ground black pepper, or more to taste

⅓ teaspoon dried sage

A pinch of ground allspice

1. Preheat the air fryer to 170 °C. Line the air fryer basket with parchment paper. 2. In a mixing bowl, stir together all the ingredients until well combined. 3. Make the marrow croquettes: Use a small biscuit scoop to drop tablespoonfuls of the marrow mixture onto a lightly floured surface and shape into balls with your

hands. Transfer them to the air fryer basket. 4. Air fry for 17 minutes until the marrow croquettes are golden brown. 5. Remove from the basket to a plate and serve warm.

Golden Pickles

Prep time: 10 minutes | Cook time: 15 minutes | Serves 4

14 dill pickles, sliced

30 g flour

⅛ teaspoon baking powder

Pinch of salt

2 tablespoons cornflour plus 3 tablespoons water

6 tablespoons panko bread crumbs

½ teaspoon paprika

Cooking spray

1. Preheat the air fryer to 200°C. 2. Drain any excess moisture out of the dill pickles on a paper towel. 3. In a bowl, combine the flour, baking powder and salt. 4. Throw in the cornflour and water mixture and combine well with a whisk. 5. Put the panko bread crumbs in a shallow dish along with the paprika. Mix thoroughly. 6. Dip the pickles in the flour batter, before coating in the bread crumbs. Spritz all the pickles with the cooking spray. 7. Transfer to the air fryer basket and air fry for 15 minutes, or until golden brown. 8. Serve immediately.

Sesame Taj Tofu

Prep time: 5 minutes | Cook time: 25 minutes | Serves 4

1 block firm tofu, pressed and cut into 1-inch thick cubes

2 tablespoons soy sauce

2 teaspoons toasted sesame seeds

1 teaspoon rice vinegar

1 tablespoon cornflour

1. Preheat the air fryer to 200°C. 2. Add the tofu, soy sauce, sesame seeds, and rice vinegar in a bowl together and mix well to coat the tofu cubes. Then cover the tofu in cornflour and put it in the air fryer basket. 3. Air fry for 25 minutes, giving the basket a shake at five-minute intervals to ensure the tofu cooks evenly. 4. Serve immediately.

Bacon Potatoes and Runner Beans

Prep time: 10 minutes | Cook time: 25 minutes | Serves 4

Oil, for spraying

900 g medium Maris Piper potatoes, quartered

100 g bacon bits

280 g fresh runner beans

1 teaspoon salt

½ teaspoon freshly ground black pepper

1. Line the air fryer basket with parchment and spray lightly with oil. 2. Place the potatoes in the prepared basket. Top with the bacon bits and runner beans. Sprinkle with the salt and black pepper and spray liberally with oil. 3. Air fry at 180°C for 25 minutes, stirring after 12 minutes and spraying with oil, until the potatoes are easily pierced with a fork.

Banger-Stuffed Mushroom Caps

Prep time: 10 minutes | Cook time: 8 minutes | Serves 2

6 large portobello mushroom caps

230 g Italian banger

15 g chopped onion

2 tablespoons blanched finely ground almond flour

20 g grated Parmesan cheese

1 teaspoon minced fresh garlic

1. Use a spoon to hollow out each mushroom cap, reserving scrapings. 2. In a medium frying pan over medium heat, brown the banger about 10 minutes or until fully cooked and no pink remains. Drain and then add reserved mushroom scrapings, onion, almond flour, Parmesan, and garlic. Gently fold ingredients together and continue cooking an additional minute, then remove from heat. 3. Evenly spoon the mixture into mushroom caps and place the caps into a 6-inch round pan. Place pan into the air fryer basket. 4. Adjust the temperature to 190°C and set the timer for 8 minutes. 5. When finished cooking, the tops will be browned and bubbling. Serve warm.

Simple Cougette Crisps

Prep time: 5 minutes | Cook time: 14 minutes | Serves 4

2 courgette, sliced into ¼- to ½-inch-thick rounds

¼ teaspoon garlic granules

⅛ teaspoon sea salt

Freshly ground black pepper, to taste (optional)

Cooking spray

1. Preheat the air fryer to 200°C. Spritz the air fryer basket with cooking spray. 2. Put the courgette rounds in the air fryer basket, spreading them out as much as possible. Top with a sprinkle of garlic granules, sea salt, and black pepper (if desired). Spritz the courgette rounds with cooking spray. 3. Roast for 14 minutes, flipping the courgette rounds halfway through, or until the courgette rounds are crisp-tender. 4. Let them rest for 5 minutes and serve.

Glazed Sweet Potato Bites

Prep time: 10 minutes | Cook time: 25 minutes | Serves 4

Oil, for spraying

3 medium sweet potatoes, peeled and cut into 1-inch

pieces

2 tablespoons honey

1 tablespoon olive oil

2 teaspoons ground cinnamon

1. Line the air fryer basket with parchment and spray lightly with oil. 2. In a large bowl, toss together the sweet potatoes, honey, olive oil, and cinnamon until evenly coated. 3. Place the potatoes in the prepared basket. 4. Air fry at 200ºC for 20 to 25 minutes, or until crispy and easily pierced with a fork.

Green Peas with Mint

Prep time: 5 minutes | Cook time: 5 minutes | Serves 4

75 g shredded lettuce

1 (280 g) package frozen green peas, thawed

1 tablespoon fresh mint, shredded

1 teaspoon melted butter

1. Lay the shredded lettuce in the air fryer basket. 2. Toss together the peas, mint, and melted butter and spoon over the lettuce. 3. Air fry at 180 º C for 5 minutes, until peas are warm and lettuce wilts.

Rosemary New Potatoes

Prep time: 10 minutes | Cook time: 5 to 6 minutes | Serves 4

3 large red potatoes

¼ teaspoon ground rosemary

¼ teaspoon ground thyme

⅛ teaspoon salt

⅛ teaspoon ground black pepper

2 teaspoons extra-light olive oil

1. Preheat the air fryer to 170ºC. 2. Place potatoes in large bowl and sprinkle with rosemary, thyme, salt, and pepper. 3. Stir with a spoon to distribute seasonings

evenly. 4. Add oil to potatoes and stir again to coat well. 5. Air fry at 170ºC for 4 minutes. Stir and break apart any that have stuck together. 6. Cook an additional 1 to 2 minutes or until fork-tender.

Green Tomato Salad

Prep time: 10 minutes | Cook time: 8 to 10 minutes | Serves 4

4 green tomatoes

½ teaspoon salt

1 large egg, lightly beaten

50 g peanut flour

1 tablespoon Creole seasoning

1 (140 g) bag rocket

Buttermilk Dressing:

230 g mayonnaise

120 g sour cream

2 teaspoons fresh lemon juice

2 tablespoons finely chopped fresh parsley

1 teaspoon dried dill

1 teaspoon dried chives

½ teaspoon salt

½ teaspoon garlic powder

½ teaspoon onion powder

1. Preheat the air fryer to 200ºC. 2. Slice the tomatoes into ½-inch slices and sprinkle with the salt. Let sit for 5 to 10 minutes. 3. Place the egg in a small shallow bowl. In another small shallow bowl, combine the peanut flour and Creole seasoning. Dip each tomato slice into the egg wash, then dip into the peanut flour mixture, turning to coat evenly. 4. Working in batches if necessary, arrange the tomato slices in a single layer in the air fryer basket and spray both sides lightly with olive oil. Air fry until browned and crisp, 8 to 10 minutes. 5. To make the buttermilk dressing: In a small

bowl, whisk together the mayonnaise, sour cream, lemon juice, parsley, dill, chives, salt, garlic powder, and onion powder. 6. Serve the tomato slices on top of a bed of the rocket with the dressing on the side.

Blackened Courgette with Kimchi-Herb Sauce

Prep time: 10 minutes | Cook time: 15 minutes | Serves 2

2 medium courgettes, ends trimmed (about 170 g each)

2 tablespoons olive oil

75 g kimchi, finely chopped

5 g finely chopped fresh coriander

5 g finely chopped fresh flat-leaf parsley, plus more for garnish

2 tablespoons rice vinegar

2 teaspoons Asian chili-garlic sauce

1 teaspoon grated fresh ginger

coarse sea salt and freshly ground black pepper, to taste

1. Brush the courgettes with half of the olive oil, place in the air fryer, and air fry at 200°C, turning halfway through, until lightly charred on the outside and tender, about 15 minutes. 2. Meanwhile, in a small bowl, combine the remaining 1 tablespoon olive oil, the kimchi, coriander, parsley, vinegar, chili-garlic sauce, and ginger. 3. Once the courgette is finished cooking, transfer it to a colander and let it cool for 5 minutes. Using your fingers, pinch and break the courgette into bite-size pieces, letting them fall back into the colander. Season the courgette with salt and pepper, toss to combine, then let sit a further 5 minutes to allow some of its liquid to drain. Pile the courgette atop the kimchi sauce on a plate and sprinkle with more parsley to serve.

Spiced Butternut Marrow

Prep time: 10 minutes | Cook time: 15 minutes | Serves 4

600 g 1-inch-cubed butternut marrow

2 tablespoons vegetable oil

1 to 2 tablespoons brown sugar

1 teaspoon Chinese five-spice powder

1. In a medium bowl, combine the marrow, oil, sugar, and five-spice powder. Toss to coat. 2. Place the marrow in the air fryer basket. Set the air fryer to 200°C for 15 minutes or until tender.

Blistered Shishito Peppers with Lime Juice

Prep time: 5 minutes | Cook time: 9 minutes | Serves 3

230 g shishito peppers, rinsed

Cooking spray

Sauce:

1 tablespoon tamari or shoyu

2 teaspoons fresh lime juice

2 large garlic cloves, minced

1. Preheat the air fryer to 200°C. Spritz the air fryer basket with cooking spray. 2. Place the shishito peppers in the basket and spritz them with cooking spray. Roast for 3 minutes. 3. Meanwhile, whisk together all the ingredients for the sauce in a large bowl. Set aside. 4. Shake the basket and spritz them with cooking spray again, then roast for an additional 3 minutes. 5. Shake the basket one more time and spray the peppers with cooking spray. Continue roasting for 3 minutes until the peppers are blistered and nicely browned. 6. Remove the peppers from the basket to the bowl of sauce. Toss to coat well and serve immediately.

Curry Roasted Cauliflower

Prep time: 10 minutes | Cook time: 20 minutes | Serves 4

65 ml olive oil

2 teaspoons curry powder

½ teaspoon salt

¼ teaspoon freshly ground black pepper

1 head cauliflower, cut into bite-size florets

½ red onion, sliced

2 tablespoons freshly chopped parsley, for garnish (optional)

1. Preheat the air fryer to 200°C. 2. In a large bowl, combine the olive oil, curry powder, salt, and pepper. Add the cauliflower and onion. Toss gently until the vegetables are completely coated with the oil mixture. Transfer the vegetables to the basket of the air fryer. 3. Pausing about halfway through the cooking time to shake the basket, air fry for 20 minutes until the cauliflower is tender and beginning to brown. Top with the parsley, if desired, before serving.

Lemon-Garlic Mushrooms

Prep time: 10 minutes | Cook time: 10 to 15 minutes | Serves 6

340 g sliced mushrooms

1 tablespoon avocado oil

Sea salt and freshly ground black pepper, to taste

3 tablespoons unsalted butter

1 teaspoon minced garlic

1 teaspoon freshly squeezed lemon juice

½ teaspoon red pepper flakes

2 tablespoons chopped fresh parsley

1. Place the mushrooms in a medium bowl and toss with the oil. Season to taste with salt and pepper. 2.

Place the mushrooms in a single layer in the air fryer basket. Set your air fryer to 190°C and roast for 10 to 15 minutes, until the mushrooms are tender. 3. While the mushrooms cook, melt the butter in a small pot or frying pan over medium-low heat. Stir in the garlic and cook for 30 seconds. Remove the pot from the heat and stir in the lemon juice and red pepper flakes. 4. Toss the mushrooms with the lemon-garlic butter and garnish with the parsley before serving.

Stuffed Red Peppers with Herbed Ricotta and Tomatoes

Prep time: 10 minutes | Cook time: 20 minutes | Serves 4

2 red peppers

250 g cooked brown rice

2 plum tomatoes, diced

1 garlic clove, minced

¼ teaspoon salt

¼ teaspoon black pepper

115 g ricotta

3 tablespoons fresh basil, chopped

3 tablespoons fresh oregano, chopped

20 g shredded Parmesan, for topping

1. Preheat the air fryer to 180°C. 2. Cut the peppers in half and remove the seeds and stem. 3. In a medium bowl, combine the brown rice, tomatoes, garlic, salt, and pepper. 4. Distribute the rice filling evenly among the four pepper halves. 5. In a small bowl, combine the ricotta, basil, and oregano. Put the herbed cheese over the top of the rice mixture in each pepper. 6. Place the peppers into the air fryer and roast for 20 minutes. 7. Remove and serve with shredded Parmesan on top.

Mashed Sweet Potato Tots

Prep time: 10 minutes | Cook time: 12 to 13 minutes per batch | Makes 18 to 24 tots

- 210 g cooked mashed sweet potatoes
- 1 egg white, beaten
- ⅛ teaspoon ground cinnamon
- 1 dash nutmeg
- 2 tablespoons chopped pecans
- 1½ teaspoons honey
- Salt, to taste
- 50 g panko bread crumbs
- Oil for misting or cooking spray

1. Preheat the air fryer to 200°C. 2. In a large bowl, mix together the potatoes, egg white, cinnamon, nutmeg, pecans, honey, and salt to taste. 3. Place panko crumbs on a sheet of wax paper. 4. For each tot, use about 2 teaspoons of sweet potato mixture. To shape, drop the measure of potato mixture onto panko crumbs and push crumbs up and around potatoes to coat edges. Then turn tot over to coat other side with crumbs. 5. Mist tots with oil or cooking spray and place in air fryer basket in single layer. 6. Air fry at 200°C for 12 to 13 minutes, until browned and crispy. 7. Repeat steps 5 and 6 to cook remaining tots.

Chapter 9 Vegetarian Mains

Mushroom and Pepper Pizza Squares

Prep time: 10 minutes | Cook time: 10 minutes | Serves 10

1 pizza dough, cut into squares

235 g chopped oyster mushrooms

1 shallot, chopped

¼ red pepper, chopped

2 tablespoons parsley

Salt and ground black pepper, to taste

1. Preheat the air fryer to 200°C. 2.In a bowl, combine the oyster mushrooms, shallot, pepper and parsley. 3.Sprinkle some salt and pepper as desired. 4.Spread this mixture on top of the pizza squares. 5.Bake in the air fryer for 10 minutes. 6.Serve warm.

Spinach-Artichoke Stuffed Mushrooms

Prep time: 10 minutes | Cook time: 10 to 14 minutes | Serves 4

2 tablespoons olive oil

4 large portobello mushrooms, stems removed and gills scraped out

½ teaspoon salt

¼ teaspoon freshly ground pepper

110 g goat cheese, crumbled

120 g chopped marinated artichoke hearts

235 g frozen spinach, thawed and squeezed dry

120 g grated Parmesan cheese

2 tablespoons chopped fresh parsley

1. Preheat the air fryer to 200°C. 2.Rub the olive oil over the portobello mushrooms until thoroughly coated. 3.Sprinkle both sides with the salt and black pepper. 4.Place top-side down on a clean work surface. 5.In a small bowl, combine the goat cheese, artichoke hearts, and spinach. 6.Mash with the back of a fork until thoroughly combined. 7.Divide the cheese mixture among the mushrooms and sprinkle with the Parmesan cheese. 8.Air fry for 10 to 14 minutes until the mushrooms are tender and the cheese has begun to brown. 9.Top with the fresh parsley just before serving.

Aubergine Parmesan

Prep time: 15 minutes | Cook time: 17 minutes | Serves 4

1 medium aubergine, ends trimmed, sliced into ½ -inch rounds

¼ teaspoon salt

2 tablespoons coconut oil

120 g grated Parmesan cheese

30 g cheese crisps, finely crushed

120 ml low-carb marinara sauce

120 g shredded Mozzarella cheese

1. Sprinkle aubergine rounds with salt on both sides and wrap in a kitchen towel for 30 minutes. 2.Press to remove excess water, then drizzle rounds with coconut oil on both sides. 3.In a medium bowl, mix Parmesan and cheese crisps. 4.Press each aubergine slice into mixture to coat both sides. 5.Place rounds into ungreased air fryer basket. 6.Adjust the temperature to 180 °C and air fry for 15 minutes, turning rounds halfway through cooking. 7.They will be crispy around the edges when done. 8.Spoon marinara over rounds and sprinkle with Mozzarella. 9.Continue cooking an additional 2 minutes at 180°C until cheese is melted. 10.Serve warm.

Vegetable Burgers

Prep time: 10 minutes | Cook time: 12 minutes | Serves 4

227 g cremini or chestnut mushrooms

2 large egg yolks

½ medium courgette, trimmed and chopped

60 g peeled and chopped brown onion

1 clove garlic, peeled and finely minced

½ teaspoon salt

¼ teaspoon ground black pepper

1. Place all ingredients into a food processor and pulse twenty times until finely chopped and combined. 2.Separate mixture into four equal sections and press each into a burger shape. 3.Place burgers into ungreased air fryer basket. 4.Adjust the temperature to 190 °C and air fry for 12 minutes, turning burgers halfway through cooking. 5.Burgers will be browned and firm when done. 6.Place burgers on a large plate and let cool 5 minutes before serving.

Gold Ravioli

Prep time: 10 minutes | Cook time: 6 minutes | Serves 4

120 g panko breadcrumbs

2 teaspoons Engevita yeast flakes

1 teaspoon dried basil

1 teaspoon dried oregano

1 teaspoon garlic powder

Salt and ground black pepper, to taste

60 g aquafaba or egg alternative

227 g ravioli

Cooking spray

1. Cover the air fryer basket with aluminium foil and coat with a light brushing of oil. 2.Preheat the air fryer to 200ºC. 3.Combine the panko breadcrumbs, Engevita yeast flakes, basil, oregano, and garlic powder. 4.Sprinkle with salt and pepper to taste. 5.Put the aquafaba in a separate bowl. 6.Dip the ravioli in the aquafaba before coating it in the panko mixture. 7.Spritz with cooking spray and transfer to the air fryer. 8.Air fry for 6 minutes. 9.Shake the air fryer basket halfway. 10.Serve hot.

Russet Potato Gratin

Prep time: 10 minutes | Cook time: 35 minutes | Serves 6

120 ml milk

7 medium russet or Maris Piper potatoes, peeled

Salt, to taste

1 teaspoon black pepper

120 ml double cream

120 g grated semi-mature cheese

½ teaspoon nutmeg

1. Preheat the air fryer to 200 °C. 2.Cut the potatoes into wafer-thin slices. 3.In a bowl, combine the milk and cream and sprinkle with salt, pepper, and nutmeg. 4.Use the milk mixture to coat the slices of potatoes. 5.Put in a baking dish. 6.Top the potatoes with the rest of the milk mixture. 7.Put the baking dish into the air fryer basket and bake for 25 minutes. 8.Pour the cheese over the potatoes. 9.Bake for an additional 10 minutes, ensuring the top is nicely browned before serving.

Loaded Cauliflower Steak

Prep time: 5 minutes | Cook time: 7 minutes | Serves 4

1 medium head cauliflower

60 ml hot sauce

2 tablespoons salted butter, melted

60 g blue cheese, crumbled

60 g full-fat ranch dressing

1. Remove cauliflower leaves. Slice the head in ½-inch-thick slices. In a small bowl, mix hot sauce and butter. Brush the mixture over the cauliflower. 2.Place each cauliflower steak into the air fryer, working in batches if necessary. 3.Adjust the temperature to 200ºC and air fry for 7 minutes. 4.When cooked, edges will begin turning dark and caramelized. To serve, sprinkle steaks with crumbled blue cheese. 5.Drizzle with ranch dressing.

Greek Baked Beans

Prep time: 5 minutes | Cook time: 30 minutes | Serves 4

Olive oil cooking spray

1 (425 g) can cannellini beans, drained and rinsed

1 (425 g) can butter beans, drained and rinsed

½ brown onion, diced

1 (230 g) can tomato sauce

1½ tablespoons raw honey

60 ml olive oil

2 garlic cloves, minced

2 tablespoons chopped fresh dill

½ teaspoon salt

½ teaspoon black pepper

1 bay leaf

1 tablespoon balsamic vinegar

60 g feta cheese, crumbled, for serving

1. Preheat the air fryer to 182°C. 2. Lightly coat the inside of a 1.2 L capacity casserole dish with olive oil cooking spray. (The shape of the casserole dish will depend upon the size of the air fryer, but it needs to be able to hold at least 1.2 L.) 3. In a large bowl, combine all ingredients except the feta cheese and stir until well combined. 4. Pour the bean mixture into the prepared casserole dish. 5. Bake in the air fryer for 30 minutes. 6. Remove from the air fryer and remove and discard the bay leaf. 7. Sprinkle crumbled feta over the top before serving.

Baked Courgette

Prep time: 10 minutes | Cook time: 8 minutes | Serves 4

2 tablespoons salted butter

60 g diced white onion

½ teaspoon minced garlic

120 ml double cream

60 g full fat soft white cheese

235 g shredded extra mature Cheddar cheese

2 medium courgette, spiralized

1. In a large saucepan over medium heat, melt butter. 2.Add onion and sauté until it begins to soften, 1 to 3 minutes. 3.Add garlic and sauté for 30 seconds, then pour in cream and add soft white cheese. 4.Remove the pan from heat and stir in Cheddar. 5.Add the courgette and toss in the sauce, then put into a round baking dish. 6.Cover the dish with foil and place into the air fryer basket. 7.Adjust the temperature to 190°C and set the timer for 8 minutes. 8.After 6 minutes remove the foil and let the top brown for remaining cooking time. 9.Stir and serve.

Roasted White Beans with Peppers

Prep time: 5 minutes | Cook time: 15 minutes | Serves 4

Olive oil cooking spray

2 (425 g) cans white beans, or cannellini beans, drained and rinsed

1 red pepper, diced

½ red onion, diced

3 garlic cloves, minced

1 tablespoon olive oil

¼ to ½ teaspoon salt

½ teaspoon black pepper

1 rosemary sprig

1 bay leaf

1. Preheat the air fryer to 182°C. 2. Lightly coat the inside of a 1.2 L capacity casserole dish with olive oil cooking spray. (The shape of the casserole dish will depend upon the size of the air fryer, but it needs to be able to hold at least 1.2 L.) 3. In a large bowl, combine the beans, red pepper, onion, garlic, olive oil, salt, and pepper. 4. Pour the bean mixture into the prepared casserole dish, place the rosemary and bay leaf on top, and then place the casserole dish into the air fryer. 5. Roast for 15 minutes. 6. Remove the rosemary and bay leaves, then stir well before serving.

Chapter 10 Desserts

Coconut-Custard Pie

Prep time: 10 minutes | Cook time: 20 to 23 minutes | Serves 4

240 ml milk

40 g granulated sugar, plus 2 tablespoons

30 g scone mix

1 teaspoon vanilla extract

2 eggs

2 tablespoons melted butter

Cooking spray

50 g desiccated coconut

1. Place all ingredients except coconut in a medium bowl. 2. Using a hand mixer, beat on high speed for 3 minutes. 3. Let sit for 5 minutes. 4. Preheat the air fryer to 160°C. 5. Spray a baking pan with cooking spray and place pan in air fryer basket. 6. Pour filling into pan and sprinkle coconut over top. 7. Cook pie for 20 to 23 minutes or until center sets.

Olive Oil Cake

Prep time: 10 minutes | Cook time: 30 minutes | Serves 8

60 g blanched finely ground almond flour

5 large eggs, whisked

175 ml extra-virgin olive oil

75 g granulated sweetener

1 teaspoon vanilla extract

1 teaspoon baking powder

1. In a large bowl, mix all ingredients. Pour batter into an ungreased round nonstick baking dish. 2. Place dish into air fryer basket. Adjust the temperature to 150°C and bake for 30 minutes. The cake will be golden on top and firm in the center when done. 3. Let cake cool in dish 30 minutes before slicing and serving.

Baked Brazilian Pineapple

Prep time: 10 minutes | Cook time: 10 minutes | Serves 4

60 g brown sugar

2 teaspoons ground cinnamon

1 small pineapple, peeled, cored, and cut into spears

3 tablespoons unsalted butter, melted

1. In a small bowl, mix the brown sugar and cinnamon until thoroughly combined. 2. Brush the pineapple spears with the melted butter. Sprinkle the cinnamon-sugar over the spears, pressing lightly to ensure it adheres well. 3. Place the spears in the air fryer basket in a single layer. (Depending on the size of your air fryer, you may have to do this in batches.) Set the air fryer to 200°C and cook for 10 minutes for the first batch (6 to 8 minutes for the next batch, as the fryer will be preheated). Halfway through the cooking time, brush the spears with butter. 4. The pineapple spears are done when they are heated through, and the sugar is bubbling. Serve hot.

5-Ingredient Brownies

Prep time: 10 minutes | Cook time: 25 minutes | Serves 6

Vegetable oil

110 g unsalted butter

½ cup chocolate crisps

3 large eggs

80 g granulated sugar

1 teaspoon pure vanilla extract

1. Generously grease a baking pan with vegetable oil. 2.

In a microwave-safe bowl, combine the butter and chocolate crisps. Microwave on high for 1 minute. Stir very well. (You want the heat from the butter and chocolate to melt the remaining clumps. If you microwave until everything melts, the chocolate will be overcooked. If necessary, microwave for an additional 10 seconds, but stir well before you try that.) 3. In a medium bowl, combine the eggs, sugar, and vanilla. Whisk until light and frothy. Whisking continuously, slowly pour in the melted chocolate in a thin stream and whisk until everything is incorporated. 4. Pour the batter into the prepared pan. Set the pan in the air fryer basket. Set the air fryer to 180ºC, and bake for 25 minutes, or until a toothpick inserted into the center comes out clean. 5. Let cool in the pan on a wire rack for 30 minutes before cutting into squares.

Ricotta Lemon Poppy Seed Cake

Prep time: 10 minutes | Cook time: 55 minutes | Serves 4

Unsalted butter, at room temperature

55 g almond flour

80 g granulated sugar

3 large eggs

55 g double cream

60 g full-fat ricotta cheese

55 g coconut oil, melted

2 tablespoons poppy seeds

1 teaspoon baking powder

1 teaspoon pure lemon extract

Grated zest and juice of 1 lemon, plus more zest for garnish

1. Generously butter a baking pan. Line the bottom of the pan with baking paper cut to fit. 2. In a large bowl, combine the almond flour, sugar, eggs, cream, ricotta, coconut oil, poppy seeds, baking powder, lemon

extract, lemon zest, and lemon juice. Beat with a hand mixer on medium speed, until well blended and fluffy. 3. Pour the batter into the prepared pan. Cover the pan tightly with aluminium foil. Set the pan in the air fryer basket. Set the air fryer to 160 º C and cook for 45 minutes. Remove the foil and cook for 10 to 15 minutes more, until a knife (do not use a toothpick) inserted into the center of the cake comes out clean. 4. Let the cake cool in the pan on a wire rack for 10 minutes. Remove the cake from pan and let it cool on the rack for 15 minutes before slicing. 5. Top with additional lemon zest, slice and serve.

Cherry Pie

Prep time: 15 minutes | Cook time: 35 minutes | Serves 6

All-purpose flour, for dusting

1 package of shortcrust pastry, cut in half, at room temperature

350 g tin cherry pie filling

1 egg

1 tablespoon water

1 tablespoon sugar

1. Dust a work surface with flour and place the piecrust on it. Roll out the piecrust. Invert a shallow air fryer baking pan, or your own pie dish that fits inside the air fryer basket, on top of the dough. Trim the dough around the pan, making your cut ½ inch wider than the pan itself. 2. Repeat with the second piecrust but make the cut the same size as or slightly smaller than the pan. 3. Put the larger crust in the bottom of the baking pan. Don't stretch the dough. Gently press it into the pan. 4. Spoon in enough cherry pie filling to fill the crust. Do not overfill. 5. Using a knife or pizza cutter, cut the second piecrust into 1-inch-wide strips. Weave the strips in a lattice pattern over the top of the cherry pie filling. 6. Insert the crisper plate into the basket and the basket into the unit. Preheat to 160ºC. 7.

In a small bowl, whisk the egg and water. Gently brush the egg wash over the top of the pie. Sprinkle with the sugar and cover the pie with aluminium foil. 8. Once the unit is preheated, place the pie into the basket. 9. Bake for 30 minutes, remove the foil and resume cooking for 3 to 5 minutes more. The finished pie should have a flaky golden-brown crust and bubbling pie filling. 10. When the cooking is complete, serve warm. Refrigerate leftovers for a few days.

Cream-Filled Sponge Cakes

Prep time: 10 minutes | Cook time: 10 minutes | Makes 4 cakes

Coconut, or avocado oil, for spraying

1 tube croissant dough

4 Swiss rolls

1 tablespoon icing sugar

1. Line the air fryer basket with baking paper, and spray lightly with oil. 2. Unroll the dough into a single flat layer and cut it into 4 equal pieces. 3. Place 1 sponge cake in the center of each piece of dough. Wrap the dough around the cake, pinching the ends to seal. 4. Place the wrapped cakes in the prepared basket, and spray lightly with oil. 5. Bake at 90°C for 5 minutes, flip, spray with oil, and cook for another 5 minutes, or until golden brown. 6. Dust with the icing sugar and serve.

Crustless Peanut Butter Cheesecake

Prep time: 10 minutes | Cook time: 10 minutes | Serves 2

110 g cream cheese, softened

2 tablespoons powdered sweetener

1 tablespoon all-natural, no-sugar-added peanut butter

½ teaspoon vanilla extract

1 large egg, whisked

1. In a medium bowl, mix cream cheese and sweetener until smooth. Add peanut butter and vanilla, mixing until smooth. Add egg and stir just until combined. 2. Spoon mixture into an ungreased springform pan and place into air fryer basket. Adjust the temperature to 150°C and bake for 10 minutes. Edges will be firm, but center will be mostly set with only a small amount of jiggle when done. 3. Let pan cool at room temperature 30 minutes, cover with cling film, then place into refrigerator at least 2 hours. Serve chilled.

Pineapple Galette

Prep time: 15 minutes | Cook time: 40 minutes | Serves 2

¼ medium-size pineapple, peeled, cored, and cut crosswise into ¼-inch-thick slices

2 tablespoons dark rum, or apple juice

1 teaspoon vanilla extract

½ teaspoon kosher, or coarse sea salt

Finely grated zest of ½ lime

1 store-bought sheet puff pastry, cut into an 8-inch round

3 tablespoons granulated sugar

2 tablespoons unsalted butter, cubed and chilled

Coconut ice cream, for serving

1. In a small bowl, combine the pineapple slices, rum, vanilla, salt, and lime zest and let stand for at least 10 minutes to allow the pineapple to soak in the rum. 2. Meanwhile, press the puff pastry round into the bottom and up the sides of a cake pan and use the tines of a fork to dock the bottom and sides. 3. Arrange the pineapple slices on the bottom of the pastry in a more or less single layer, then sprinkle with the sugar and dot with the butter. Drizzle with the leftover juices from the bowl. Place the pan in the air fryer and bake at 150°C until the pastry is puffed and golden brown

and the pineapple is lightly caramelized on top, about 40 minutes. 4. Transfer the pan to a wire rack to cool for 15 minutes. Unmould the galette from the pan and serve warm with coconut ice cream.

Pecan Bars

Prep time: 5 minutes | Cook time: 40 minutes | Serves 12

110 g coconut flour

5 tablespoons granulated sweetener

4 tablespoons coconut oil, softened

60 ml double cream

1 egg, beaten

4 pecans, chopped

1. Mix coconut flour, sweetener, coconut oil, double cream, and egg. 2. Pour the batter in the air fryer basket and flatten well. 3. Top the mixture with pecans and cook the meal at 180°C for 40 minutes. 4. Cut the cooked meal into the bars.

Appendix: Recipe Index

Air Fried Beef Satay with Peanut Dipping Sauce----------37

Air Fried Courgette Sticks----------------------------------19

Air Fried Shishito Peppers------------------------------- 20

Almond and Caraway Crust Steak----------------------------35

Apple Cider Doughnut Holes------------------------------------5

Apple Pie Egg Rolls------------------------------------ 14

Asian Swordfish-- 46

Aubergine Parmesan--------------------------------------- 72

Bacon Eggs on the Go-- 8

Bacon Potatoes and Runner Beans---------------------------67

Bacon, Broccoli and Cheese Bread Pudding----------------11

Baked Brazilian Pineapple------------------------------------76

Baked Cheese Sandwich-----------------------------------18

Baked Chorizo Scotch Eggs-------------------------------19

Baked Courgette--74

Baked Potato Breakfast Boats--------------------------------- 7

Banger and Peppers-- 41

Banger-Stuffed Mushroom Caps------------------------------67

Barbecue Ribs---44

Beef and Pork Banger Meatloaf-------------------------------- 43

Berry Cheesecake--- 17

Black Cod with Grapes and Kale---------------------------- 55

Blackened Chicken-- 24

Blackened Courgette with Kimchi-Herb Sauce------------69

Blistered Shishito Peppers with Lime Juice---------------69

Blueberry Cobbler---12

Bone-in Pork Chops------------------------------------- 41

Bourbon Vanilla Eggy Bread--------------------------------- 12

Brazilian Tempero Baiano Chicken Drumsticks-----------27

Breakfast Meatballs--------------------------------------- 7

Broccoli Cheese Chicken----------------------------------- 21

Bruschetta with Basil Pesto----------------------------- 62

Buffalo Chicken Cheese Sticks------------------------------ 31

Butter and Bacon Chicken--------------------------------- 25

Buttermilk Breaded Chicken--------------------------------28

Butternut Marrow Croquettes------------------------------66

Cajun and Lemon Pepper Cod-----------------------------52

Cajun Salmon--- 45

Cajun-Breaded Chicken Bites-------------------------------- 30

Canadian Bacon Muffin Sandwiches------------------------- 6

Caraway Crusted Beef Steaks--------------------------------43

Catfish Bites--- 54

Cauliflower Steaks Gratin--------------------------------- 64

Cheddar Eggs---13

Cheese-Stuffed Blooming Onion-------------------------- 60

Cheesy Baked Coarse Cornmeal---------------------------- 20

Cheesy Courgette Tots------------------------------------- 56

Cherry Pie--- 77

Chicken and Avocado Fajitas------------------------------21

Chicken and Broccoli Casserole----------------------------23

Chicken Burgers with Gammon and Cheese--------------- 22

Chicken Shawarma--------------------------------------- 22

Chinese-Inspired Spareribs-------------------------------- 16

Chinese-Style Pork Loin Back Ribs------------------------ 35

Classic Whole Chicken--23

Coconut Chicken Meatballs-------------------------------23

Coconut Prawns with Pineapple-Lemon Sauce-----------45

Coconut-Custard Pie----------------------------------- 76

Coriander Lime Chicken Thighs----------------------------31

Crab Cakes--- 46

Cream-Filled Sponge Cakes----------------------------- 78

Crispy Chilli Chickpeas----------------------------------- 59

Crispy Fish Fingers----------------------------------- 51

Crustless Peanut Butter Cheesecake----------------------78

Curry Roasted Cauliflower----------------------------- 70

Denver Omelette--13

Easy Beef Satay--------------------------------------- 39

Easy Cajun Chicken Drumsticks----------------------------28

Easy Chicken Nachos------------------------------------21

Easy Devils on Horseback----------------------------- 18

Easy Turkey Tenderloin--------------------------------- 27

Egg Roll Pizza Sticks----------------------------------- 58

Egg Tarts--8

Eggnog Bread--- 10

Fajita Meatball Lettuce Wraps----------------------------- 40

Firecracker Prawns----------------------------------- 51

Fish and Vegetable Tacos------------------------------- 15

Fried Green Tomatoes--------------------------------- 17

Fried Prawns--- 52

Garlic Balsamic London Broil------------------------- 35

Garlic Roasted Broccoli------------------------------- 64

Garlic-Roasted Tomatoes and Olives----------------------63

Glazed Sweet Potato Bites--------------------------------- 67

Gluten-Free Muesli Cereal----------------------------- 11

Goat Cheese and Garlic Crostini----------------------------- 56

Gold Livers--- 31

Gold Ravioli---73

Golden Avocado Tempura----------------------------------5

Golden Onion Rings-----------------------------------59

Golden Pickles--- 66

Golden Salmon and Carrot Croquettes----------------------57

Greek Baked Beans----------------------------------- 74

Greek Fish Pitas---48

Greek Potato Skins with Olives and Feta------------------58

Green Eggs and Gammon----------------------------------- 6

Green Peas with Mint-----------------------------------68

Green Tomato Salad----------------------------------- 68

Greens Crisps with Curried Yoghurt Sauce---------------- 61

Grilled Gammon and Cheese on Raisin Bread------------63

Herb-Roasted Veggies----------------------------------- 19

Hoisin BBQ Pork Chops----------------------------------37

Honey-Baked Pork Loin----------------------------------35

Indian Mint and Chile Kebabs------------------------- 43

Italian Chicken with Sauce----------------------------------30

Italian Pork Loin--- 36

Jalapeño Popper Egg Cups----------------------------- 12

Jalapeño Popper Hasselback Chicken--------------------- 28

Jalapeño Popper Pork Chops----------------------------- 33

Juicy Paprika Chicken Breast----------------------------------32

Kale and Beef Omelet-----------------------------------40

Kale Crisps with Sesame----------------------------- 56

Keto Quiche--- 9

Kheema Burgers---38

Lebanese Muhammara----------------------------------- 57

Lemon Mahi-Mahi---48

Lemon Pepper Prawns-------------------------------------51

Lemon-Basil Turkey Breasts	28
Lemon-Dijon Boneless Chicken	29
Lemon-Garlic Mushrooms	70
Lemon-Pepper Trout	45
Lemon-Tarragon Fish en Papillote	49
Lemony Pear Chips	57
Loaded Cauliflower Steak	73
Mashed Sweet Potato Tots	70
Meatball Subs	14
Mediterranean Beef Steaks	42
Mexican Breakfast Pepper Rings	8
Minute Steak Roll-Ups	33
Mississippi Spice Muffins	5
Moroccan Spiced Halibut with Chickpea Salad	53
Mushroom and Green Bean Casserole	15
Mushroom and Pepper Pizza Squares	72
Mustard Lamb Chops	44
Nashville Hot Chicken	26
Not-So-English Muffins	7
Old Bay Tilapia	14
Olive Oil Cake	76
Panko Pork Chops	39
Paprika Crab Burgers	50
Paprika Prawns	54
Parmesan Banger Egg Muffins	8
Parmesan-Crusted Halibut Fillets	50
Parmesan-Thyme Butternut Marrow	65
Pecan Bars	79
Personal Cauliflower Pizzas	16
Pineapple Galette	78

Piri-Piri Chicken Thighs	26
Pomegranate-Glazed Chicken with Couscous Salad	25
Pork and Cabbage Egg Rolls	62
Pork and Tricolor Vegetables Kebabs	38
Pork Medallions with Endive Salad	42
Pork Tenderloin with Avocado Lime Sauce	36
Poutine with Waffle Fries	60
Prawns Curry	47
Red Pepper and Feta Frittata	9
Ricotta Lemon Poppy Seed Cake	77
Roast Beef with Horseradish Cream	34
Roasted Cod with Lemon-Garlic Potatoes	53
Roasted Fish with Almond-Lemon Crumbs	52
Roasted White Beans with Peppers	74
Rosemary New Potatoes	68
Rosemary Ribeye Steaks	37
Rosemary Roast Beef	40
Russet Potato Gratin	73
Salmon Burgers with Creamy Broccoli Slaw	46
Salmon with Fennel and Carrot	47
Saltine Wax Beans	65
Scallops with Asparagus and Peas	49
Sea Bass with Potato Scales	55
Sea Salt Potato Crisps	59
Seasoned Tuna Steaks	47
Sesame Carrots and Sugar Snap Peas	64
Sesame Taj Tofu	66
Simple Air Fried Crispy Brussels Sprouts	65
Simple and Easy Croutons	18
Simple Cougette Crisps	67

South Indian Fried Fish-------------------------------------48

Southwest Corn and Pepper Roast--------------------------- 18

Southwestern Gammon Egg Cups---------------------------- 6

Spiced Butternut Marrow-----------------------------------69

Spice-Rubbed Chicken Thighs----------------------------- 29

Spicy Rump Steak--33

Spinach and Bacon Roll-ups--------------------------------9

Spinach-Artichoke Stuffed Mushrooms-------------------- 72

Sriracha-Honey Chicken Nuggets--------------------------- 24

Steak and Vegetable Kebabs--------------------------------15

Stuffed Red Peppers with Herbed Ricotta and Tomatoes
--- 70

Supplì al Telefono (Risotto Croquettes)---------------------61

Sweet Chili Spiced Chicken----------------------------------- 24

Sweet Maize and Carrot Fritters------------------------------ 19

Tex-Mex Salmon Bowl--50

Thai-Style Cornish Game Hens------------------------------ 30

Tomato and Bacon Zoodles---------------------------------- 34

Tomato and Mozzarella Bruschetta---------------------------7

Tuna Avocado Bites---51

Turkey Banger Breakfast Pizza------------------------------- 10

Vegetable Burgers--73

Veggie Salmon Nachos--------------------------------------- 56

Zesty Fried Asparagus-- 65

Printed in Great Britain
by Amazon